JOHN LENNON

HIS LIFE AND LEGEND

RICHARD BUSKIN

PUBLICATIONS INTERNATIONAL, LTD.

Richard Buskin is a freelance music and film journalist based in London. His interviews, feature articles, and photographs have appeared in numerous publications around the world. *John Lennon: His Life and Legend* is his first book.

ACKNOWLEDGMENTS

The author would like to thank Mark Lewisohn, for his invaluable and generous assistance throughout this project; Allen J. Wiener, for his tireless efforts in helping to piece together the *real* facts; David Stark, for providing unlimited access to his Pete Shotton interview; Bill Harry, for his recollections about John's time at Art College; Paul Goresh, for his reminiscences about John's final days; and all those associated either personally or professionally with J.L., whose conversations with the author over the years appear in part within these pages.

Special Thanks to John Beznik

John Beznik has been a Beatles collector since 1978, when he bought his first sheet music. Since then, his collection has grown to include books and 45-rpm record sleeves. He has a special regard for John Lennon.

Special Thanks to Jeff Augsburger

Jeff Augsburger is co-author of *The Beatles Memorabilia Price Guide,* a photographic compilation of his vast collection of movie and record promotions, programs, and other Beatles memorabilia from the 1960s.

 Printed and bound in Yugoslavia.

8 7 6 5 4 3 2 1

ISBN 1-56173-270-2

Library of Congress Catalog Card No. 91-61372

The irreplaceable John Lennon.

CONTENTS

INTRODUCTION: SHINING ON

"If there is such a thing as genius . . . I am one, you know, and if there isn't, I don't care."

JOHN LENNON
1970
(*Rolling Stone* interview with Jann Wenner)

Opposite: The Beatles: Four lads from Liverpool who shook the world. From the start, the group's leader and prime mover was John Lennon. Instrumental in the Beatles' enormous worldwide success, he later forged a highly significant solo career. In a remarkable age, his was a remarkable life.

John Lennon, in his life: Celebrity, musician, peace activist . . .

It is one thing to be famous; to be feted by kings, flattered by colleagues and acclaimed by the masses. To consistently capture the mass imagination, on the other hand – uniting individuals from a diversity of backgrounds and cultures, with contrasting needs, desires, tastes, and views – is altogether different. John Lennon was one of the very few people during the 20th century to accomplish both on a global scale, managing to inspire as well as entertain. He was, and is, a hero to millions, and as such his name has passed into immortality.

John was the founding force behind the Beatles and, in the early days, the group's heart and soul. He was the arty one, the sharp one, the wit, the intellectual, the leader, and it was the sting in his tail that provided the band with a unique sense of identity.

In his native country he was the down-to-earth guy who made good, whereas to the rest of the world he often represented a form of eccentricity that was typically British; the one who jumped into a hotel swimming pool wearing a sweater, and then asked the Beatles' road manager to pass him a tie "because I feel undressed."

Having enjoyed the benefits of fame, however, John eventually began to feel restricted by its drawbacks. No longer prepared to conceal the more offbeat side of his character, he decided to do away with the image of the "lovable moptop." The man who had once accepted his MBE (member of the Order of the British Empire) with a smile flippantly returned it just four years later.

Bored with the trappings of success, he was looking for fresh excitement, a new direction, and he found this in his all-consuming relationship with Yoko Ono, the tiny Japanese woman who swept him off his feet and changed the course of his life. John had at last met his true soul mate – someone who shared his outlook, indulged his fancies, and encouraged him to pursue his dreams – and as his interest in the Beatles began to fade so did the band's future.

Without his creative genius the most successful act in the history of popular music could not function properly, but while Yoko's constant presence may have spelled the end for the group, it also coincided with John's emergence as an artist in his own right and on his own terms.

His solo career comprised some of his finest work, and a period of turbulence in his marriage came to a happy conclusion when the birth of a son prompted John to take an unprecedented step: For five years he devoted himself entirely to his family. Indeed, one of the great ironies of his premature death was that it came at a time when he appeared to have at last found peace within himself.

As a human being, John Lennon always stood out from the

JOHN LENNON

. . . poet, pop-culture superstar, husband and father.

crowd, and he made a deep and lasting impression on whomever he came into contact with. As an artist, perhaps his greatest talent was his ability to communicate, to touch a chord of familiarity and evoke a positive response. This enabled him to find a permanent place in people's hearts as well as their minds.

Like his audience, he was composed of disparate parts. He could be alternately tender and volatile, charming and disagreeable, caring and irresponsible, orthodox and unconventional. Perhaps in him we each saw a part of ourselves: the good, the bad, and the indifferent.

Here was an ordinary man with an extraordinary, God-given talent; a restless soul with the need and the capacity to share his innermost thoughts and experiences, his hopes, his insecurities, his highs and his lows. And he knew that we'd listen. One could disagree with John Lennon, be annoyed or disappointed with him, but it was difficult to ignore him. The sheer force of his personality saw to that.

While his actions could often be contradictory, he clearly believed in whatever he did at a particular moment. Whether he was campaigning for peace, championing a radical cause, pledging his love, or hitting out at people and principles through his songs, he had the courage and conviction to carry it through, and the basic integrity to admit when he had made a mistake.

On the one hand cynical, John frequently displayed an idealist's naivete, yet it was the basic honesty of both his written and spoken words that always won through. To listen to one of his songs is to know precisely what he meant at that moment in time. The sincerity in the music, the voice, and the lyrics is undeniable; he wasn't just singing about emotions, he was feeling them. As he told David Sheff in a 1980 *Playboy* interview, "I like to write about me, 'cos I know me."

Ever practical, he was far more interested in the days and years to come than those gone by, and his patchy memory allowed little space for nostalgic flashbacks. "I don't have any romanticism about any part of my past," he said to Sheff. "I don't believe in yesterday." At the same time, he was also immensely proud of all that he had achieved both within and without the Beatles, and he would always be the first to jump to the band's defense whenever some criticism bothered him.

By way of straightforward analysis, as well as the recollections of many who associated with John Lennon on either a personal or professional basis, this book bypasses the unfounded and the insignificant and provides an insight into the life and work of a man who, during his lifetime and beyond, has given pleasure and hope to millions.

The artistic legacy is peerless, the spirit shines on. This is his story.

CHAPTER 1

IN THE BEGINNING: 1940-1955

"Certainly on the road to failure . . . hopeless"

JOHN LENNON'S SCHOOL REPORT
c. 1955

Opposite: Never meek, John was determined from an early age to make his presence felt. As the five-year-old new boy at Dovedale Primary School, he possessed angelic looks but a mind set on mischief.

Liverpool Maternity Hospital, where John Winston Lennon was born at 6:30 p.m. on
October 9, 1940. His father, Freddie, was away at sea on the memorable day.

Never one to make a discreet entrance, when John Lennon came into the world on October 9, 1940, it was amid a Liverpool whose docks and surrounding neighborhoods were under almost constant threat from the bombs of Hitler's Luftwaffe. The Battle of Britain had moved into high gear as the Germans attempted to complete their takeover of Western Europe, but Mary Elizabeth (Mimi) Smith was prepared to risk the possibility of flying debris and shrapnel. She ran all the way to Liverpool Maternity Hospital as soon as she heard that her sister, Julia, had given birth to a baby son, christened with the middle name of Winston as a tribute to Britain's unflagging Prime Minister.

Mimi's effort to see her new nephew was rewarded for, as she asserted many years later, "I knew the moment I first set eyes on John that he was going to be something special."

Mimi's reaction displayed either great premonition or, more likely, natural favoritism. In any case, she need have looked no further than the little boy's mother to determine the broad shape of his personality.

Julia Lennon (born Stanley) was a carefree, fun-loving woman. Her behavior was sometimes irresponsible and often eccentric, and in sharp contrast to the reserved manners and sober attitude of Mimi. "She was witty and full of fun," Mimi told Beatles chronicler Hunter Davies. "She never took life or anything seriously. Everything was funny, but she couldn't see into people until it was too late. She was more sinned against than sinning."

Julia was a movie usherette before she married ship's steward Alfred (Freddie) Lennon on a whim on December 3, 1938. Both in their mid-twenties, they were at first very happy

JOHN LENNON

together, but neither of them was ready, emotionally or financially, to bring up a child.

Freddie's father, Jack, had been born in Dublin and toured the United States as a Kentucky minstrel during the 1890s. Retirement brought him to Liverpool, and after Jack's death in 1921 nine-year-old Freddie tried to continue the showbiz tradition when he ran away from his orphanage to join a children's troupe. The authorities soon put an end to his big-time ambitions, however, and by the age of 15 he was well educated and working as an office boy. It was at around this time that he met Julia Stanley.

A year later he quit the office for the sea, finding employment first as a bellboy and then as a waiter, but his lack of ambition meant that he would progress no further. By the time John was born some twelve years later, Freddie was serving as headwaiter on a ship bound for New York. The home life was not for him, and in spite of the occasional visit and the odd postcard, there was little sign of the elder Lennon over the next few years as he sailed his way around Canada, France, Italy, and North Africa.

Julia, in the meantime, was not exactly tying herself down either. Having handed over the responsibility for John's upbringing to Mimi and her husband George, she decided that the best way to mourn Freddie's absence was to go out and have a good time with her friends. For a while everything ran smoothly, but then Freddie spoiled things.

In an attempt to save the faltering marriage, he reappeared on the scene shortly after the five-year-old John had been enrolled in Dovedale Primary School off Penny Lane. Needless to say, he came back too late to do the marriage any good. His wife had set up housekeeping with another man, and she showed absolutely no interest in Freddie's desperate pleas to patch up the relationship. His response was to take John to the nearby coastal resort of Blackpool, secretly planning to emigrate with his son to New Zealand and start a new life there. Julia, sensing trouble, arrived in Blackpool and demanded that their son return to Liverpool with her. What

9 Newcastle Road, Liverpool 15, John's first home before he went to live with his Aunt Mimi and Uncle George. His mother, Julia, lived in this tiny house with her father, and spent what little married life she had with Freddie here.

JOHN LENNON

Dressed in his school blazer, eight-year-old John poses with his aunt,
Mimi Smith, in the garden of their Liverpool home.

JOHN LENNON

Cleanup time: John's father, Freddie, comes to grips with some dirty dishes in the Greyhound Hotel, Hampton Court, in 1965. At this time, the wayward Freddie had not seen his son in 20 years.

followed was a reckless tug-of-love that left emotional scars that John would carry for the rest of his life.

In a ridiculous scene straight out of the movies, the parents presented their child with an ultimatum as to whom he wanted to live with. Totally confused, the sobbing boy first opted for his father, but then, after watching his mother walk out of the door and down the street, he changed his mind and chased after her. Freddie later told Hunter Davies, author of *The Beatles: The Authorized Biography,* "That was the last I saw of him or heard of him until I was told he'd become a Beatle."

Despite his decision to be with his mother, John would not spend the remainder of his childhood living with her. Having made her point and won her battle, Julia placed her son back in the sedate and comfortable setting of Mendips, Mimi and George's house at 251 Menlove Avenue, situated in the middle-class Liverpool suburb of Woolton. Here John would spend his days playing with friends, indulging his passion for drawing and, after Uncle George had taught him how, reading books and newspapers in his small bedroom above the front porch. Among his favorite books were *Just William, Alice's Adventures in Wonderland,* and *The Wind in the Willows.* By the time he was seven he had compiled his own series of jokes, drawings, and cartoons, under the title of "Sport, Speed and Illustrated. Edited and Illustrated by J. W. Lennon." Possibly influenced by occasional outings to the cinema, each installment ended with "If you liked this, come again next week. It'll be even better."

The infrequent visits by Julia added to the household's overall feeling of stability. Looking back on this period Mimi, together with her three other sisters – Anne, Elizabeth, and

Menlove Avenue in the Liverpool suburb of Woolton. It was on this street that
John's Aunt Mimi and Uncle George kept house, and where John
spent most of his childhood.

Harriet – would recall to biographer Hunter Davies that the pre-teen John "was as happy as the day was long."

That may have been true on the surface, but John's attitude at school displayed an underlying anger and frustration, possibly because of his parents' neglect. The teachers noted his talent for art and his sharp mind, but also suffered a boy with a sharp tongue and an appetite for fighting and mischief-making.

Hunter Davies quotes John as admitting, "I fought all the way through Dovedale. I learned lots of dirty jokes very young; there was this girl who told me them. . . . Other boys' parents hated me. They were always warning their kids not to play with me."

Not that this bothered John – quite the opposite, in fact, for the boy discovered that a shabby appearance only enhanced the effect of rebelliousness. Seeing conformity as a sign of weakness, he hated the idea of a school uniform, and he made this quite clear by wearing a black blazer that often looked more like a crumpled bag, a white shirt that was usually unbuttoned, and gray shorts that would typically be covered in mud.

For the ultra-strict Mimi this kind of behavior was too much to endure. One of John's favorite stories about his aunt centered around the time she was walking down Penny Lane and saw a crowd observing a fight between a couple of "common scruffs." As recounted by Hunter Davies, Mimi confidently assumed that the battling youngsters were from one of the rougher schools in the area, but when the fists stopped flying she saw "this awful boy with his coat hanging off. To my horror, it was Lennon!"

Poor Mimi. Here she was, doing her best to bring John up "properly," and all he could do was let her down! Still, intelligence combined with a minimum of studying saw

JOHN LENNON

Dovedale Primary School, where John began studies in 1946. A painting he did here
at age 11 in 1952 later adorned the sleeve of his *Walls and Bridges* album.

him through the "11-plus" (high school entrance) test, an accomplishment that earned him a brand new bicycle, courtesy of Uncle George. In September of 1952 John turned up for his first day at Quarry Bank Grammar School. Mimi had decided against the highly respected Liverpool Institute because it was situated farther away, and besides, Quarry Bank was located in a nicer, more residential district.

"I looked at the hundreds of new kids," John told Hunter Davies, "and thought, Christ, I'll have to fight my way through all this lot!"

Helping out on this unpeaceful venture was a friend, Pete Shotton, a fuzzy-haired boy who had also made the switch from Dovedale. John, by his own admission, saw aggression as his route to popularity. Never one to simply merge into the background, he had to be the leader, the hero, the center of attention. Shotton was his loyal second-in-command, and

together they set about breaking every rule they could.

"We were always looking to get into mischief," Pete remembered in a previously unpublished interview with music researcher David Stark. "Doing things that were anti-social or anti-adult, and which we knew would shock everyone."

Swearing, smoking, fighting, and penning obscene poems and drawings were all part of the rogues' repertoire, as were other petty offenses that found their way onto the John Lennon school report: "Insolence," "cutting class," and "throwing blackboard out of window."

In the book *John Winston Lennon,* author Ray Coleman quotes Eric Oldman, John's housemaster and chemistry teacher, who remembered that "[John] was awkward, but there was something in him. It wasn't sheer wickedness, but more spirit. . . . He seemed determined not to conform to the rules. But he had a wit and a humor and ability."

JOHN LENNON

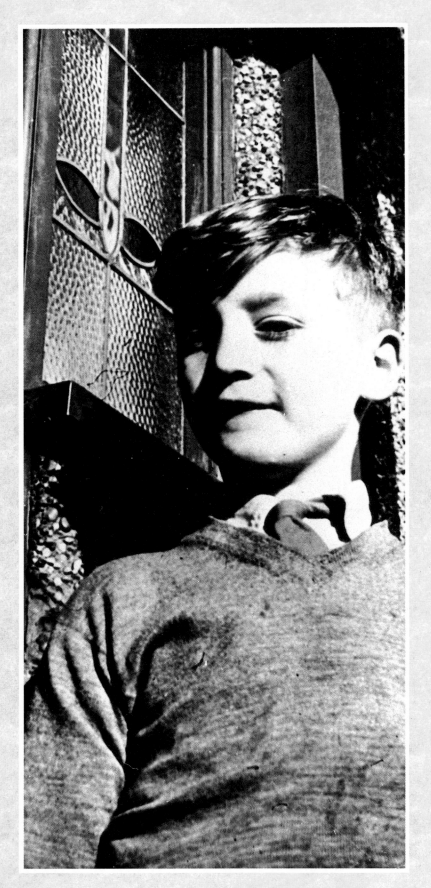

Pete Shotton recollects an incident early on during their time at Quarry Bank, when he and John were ordered to report to the Deputy Head as punishment for one of their crimes. Most kids in this kind of situation either just apologize or plead their innocence, but of course Master Lennon had to go one better. The teacher – who was sitting between the two boys – happened to be bald, and so John happily accepted the chance to perform one of his favorite tricks: tickling the man's head whenever he looked the other way. As usual, the victim tried to swat the imaginary fly, and as usual John's sleight of hand left his victim totally confused and irritated.

"I couldn't breathe, what with the laughing," Pete recalls. "It would get so that my muscles wouldn't work, I was straining my stomach so much." John showed his own amusement by quite literally wetting himself, there and then, on the spot.

"What the devil is that?" inquired the teacher, hearing a dripping noise and seeing a small puddle on the floor.

"I think the roof's leaking, sir," was John's immediate reply. Never mind the fact that it wasn't even raining!

On another occasion, the demonic duo were sent to the headmaster to be caned. While Shotton waited his turn outside the office, John went in to receive his punishment, and when he came out he was crawling on all fours, groaning. On seeing this, Pete once again couldn't control his laughter, and as a result got an even worse beating.

Canings, in fact, became part of John's staple diet, as the boy set about bullying the teachers, abandoning any form of class work, and allowing himself to slip from a strong position in the top-ranked A-stream class during the first year, to 20th in the C-stream – bottom of the bottom class – by the final term of his graduation year. Teacher Eric Oldman remarked to Lennon biographer Ray Coleman that, on John's part, "There was a simple lack of any wish to get on."

For John, indeed, academic success was irrelevant, since much of the subject matter and the method of teaching it were alien to his way of thinking. Rather than flow with the tide, he preferred to confront it head-on; at least that way he

Quarry Bank Grammar School, where John made mischief between
1952 and 1957.

Opposite: Mr. Mischief himself in May 1948, outside the home he shared with
Aunt Mimi and Uncle George.

would gain some pleasure out of the whole experience, as well as local notoriety.

"People like me are aware of their so-called genius at ten, eight, nine," he remarked to Jann Wenner during a 1970 *Rolling Stone* interview. "I always wondered, 'why has nobody discovered me?' . . . didn't they see that I'm cleverer than anybody in this school? That the teachers are stupid, too? That all they had was information that I didn't need. . . . I was different. I was always different. Why didn't anybody notice me?"

"He had a magnetism which attracted everybody," adds Shotton. "Everyone was interested in John, because even as a kid he had a great awareness about everything going on about him. He had an amazingly quick wit, a great sense of humor, an ability to turn serious situations upside down on their head and transform them into surrealistic plays. So in school and out of school people always wanted to be in his company, because he brightened everything up."

Approaching his mid-teens, John began to reestablish links with his mother, who was living less than two miles away from Mendips. Yet the renewal of one relationship coincided with the severing of another: Uncle George, the kindly ex-dairy farmer who provided the counterbalance to Mimi's strict rule – the man who would humor John while his wife was punishing him, and the one who taught his nephew to read, took him for walks, and bought him a bike – died from a hemorrhage on June 5, 1955, at the age of 52. John was on a camping holiday in Scotland at the time, and when he returned home a couple of days later and learned of the news, he felt unsure how to express his shock and pain, and withdrew to the safety of his bedroom.

"Then my cousin Leila arrived," he recalled for biographer Hunter Davies, "and she came upstairs as well. We both had hysterics. We just laughed and laughed. I felt very guilty afterwards."

JOHN LENNON

19

JOHN LENNON

An offhand reaction to a traumatic situation was typical of John Lennon, for this habit would repeat itself time and again throughout the years. On the one hand extremely outgoing, he could at the same time be emotionally withdrawn, especially when it came to betraying signs of weakness. Responding with nervous laughter or simply clamming up was his way of protecting himself against further hurt. It wouldn't be until much later in life that he would begin to confront this problem.

Now, however, with Uncle George gone, his feeling of isolation from those around him intensified, for apart from the free-and-easy Julia and his small circle of close friends, few people in his life appeared to be functioning anywhere near his wavelength.

"It's scary when you're a child," he later reflected during a *Playboy* interview with David Sheff, "because there is nobody to relate to. . . . What the hell do you do? You want to belong but you don't want to belong, because you cannot belong."

As John became more resentful of the demands of his aunt, his school, and of society in general, he drew closer to his mother, whom he regarded almost as a big sister. He would spend weekends in the suburb of Allerton, at the house Julia shared with her boyfriend, John Dykins – whose facial tic prompted the ever-sensitive John to christen him with the charming nickname of "Twitchy." Julia would join her son in ridiculing all those whom they considered to be "thickheads." But while it was easy to laugh at others, John still wasn't at all sure as to his own future.

"I didn't really know what I wanted to be, apart from ending up an eccentric millionaire," he remarked to biographer Hunter Davies. "I fancied marrying a millionairess and doing it that way. . . . If I couldn't do it without being crooked, then I'd have to be crooked. But I was too much of a coward to be a crook. I'd never have made it."

So, in spite of everyone's best efforts to tie him down, the rebellious side of John's nature had surfaced. All he needed now was a cause that would give him a sense of direction. He found it in music.

A current shot of "Mendips" in Woolton, once the home of John and Aunt Mimi and Uncle George. Today, the strategically positioned trees and shrubs block the view of fans and idle sightseers. Mimi moved from the house in 1965, when John bought her a luxury seaside bungalow on England's south coast.

Opposite: John, aged ten, stands outside Mendips; the window above the front porch belonged to his bedroom, where he would spend hours reading, writing, and, a few years later, playing his guitar.

JOHN LENNON

CHAPTER 2

ROCK 'N' ROLL!

*"It was Elvis who got me
hooked for beat music. When
I heard 'Heartbreak Hotel,'
I thought 'this is it' and
I started to grow sideburns
and all that gear."*

JOHN LENNON
1963
(*New Musical Express* interview with Alan Smith)

Opposite: The first-ever photograph of John performing live, atop a stationary
coal truck with the Quarry Men in Rosebery Street, Liverpool, on June 22, 1957.
The 16-year-old Teddy boy is at the microphone, with (left to right) Colin Hanton
on drums, Eric Griffiths on guitar, Len Garry on tea-chest bass, Pete Shotton
playing the washboard, and Rod Davis on banjo.

During his earliest years, music never really played a major part in John's life. At the age of eight he sang in the choir of St. Peter's Church near his home, but his career there came to a swift end once it was discovered that he and his friends had been eating the grapes used to decorate the church for the Harvest Festival.

Then, when John was ten, Uncle George bought him a cheap harmonica that he carried in his blazer pocket. Once, on his way to visit an aunt in Scotland, he played it throughout the bus journey. "The driver liked it and told me to meet him at a place in Edinburgh the next morning, and he'd give me a good mouth organ," John recalled in an interview with *Record Mirror* in 1971. "So I went, and he gave me a fantastic one; it really got me going. I also had a little accordion which I used to play – only the right hand – and I played the same things on this that I played on the mouth organ; things like 'Swedish Rhapsody,' 'Moulin Rouge,' and 'Greensleeves.'"

At this point, he was showing just a natural child's curiosity about music; it could hardly be said that music was in his blood. Later on, during John's early teens, the first rumblings of rock 'n' roll were heard when Bill Haley and His Comets released popular records such as "Crazy Man Crazy" and "Rock Around The Clock." But Haley, a chubby-faced man with a spit curl, looked more like a parent than a teen idol, and he made very little impression on the young Lennon.

"The Bill Haley era passed me by, in a way," he said in the *Record Mirror* interview. "When his records came on the wireless, my mother would start dancing around, she thought they were so good. I used to hear them, but they didn't do anything for me."

Maybe, but the fact that he would associate memories of his mother with this era is a sign of just how close the two were becoming. John felt more and more drawn to this bubbly, red-headed woman, not only because of the way she encouraged his rebelliousness, but also because of her quirky, often eccentric sense of humor, something that he could readily identify with.

Bill Haley and His Comets found enormous success in America beginning in 1954, and were a big hit in Britain, too. John was well aware of Haley but, not surprisingly, perhaps, was not enticed by the singer's friendly, unrebellious personal image.

A collection of LPs by the five major artists who, along with Elvis Presley, totally
turned John's world around during the late fifties. He would later liken their
influence upon him to that of "primitive painters."

"[Julia] was a fabulous, fabulous woman," says Pete Shotton. "She always made us welcome when we were skiving off school, and apart from the fact that she was such good fun to have around, she was more like a friend than a mate's mother. She didn't act like a parent, she didn't talk like a parent. She made a game of everything – she would even dust the furniture moving around as if she were a ballet dancer – and the things that she did showed her eccentricity."

Among the more notable examples was the time she met the two boys in public, wearing a pair of knickers (bloomers) on her head in place of a scarf. Pete Shotton remembers, "They were the old-fashioned kind of knickers, you know, so the legs were hanging down over her back. People were staring, but she was just so cool about it, it was hysterical!

"Then there was another occasion, when we were walking along with her and she was wearing a pair of specs with no glass in the frames. No one really noticed, until she'd go up to someone she knew, start talking to them and casually rub her eye by poking her finger straight through the frame. We'd be watching all this, literally crying with laughter!"

Yet, while matters seemed to be taking a definite turn for the better in his private life, back at school John was still going nowhere fast. Showing no concern for either his studies or his future, his main interest lay in disrupting the class. There was, however, a productive side to his antics.

The homework session at the end of each day wasn't supervised by anyone, and John therefore saw this as a great chance to put his budding artistic and poetic skills to the test.

HEARTBREAK HOTEL

Words and Music by MAE BOREN AXTON, TOMMY DURDEN and ELVIS PRESLEY
AS RECORDED BY ELVIS PRESLEY FOR RCA VICTOR

ELVIS
PRESLEY

TREE PUBLISHING CO., INC.
Sole Selling Agents
KEYS MUSIC, INC.   146 W. 54th Street, New York 19, N.Y.

Sheet music for the song that redefined
popular music in 1956, and inspired
the next generation of rock artists.
"Nothing really affected me until Elvis,"
John would later say. "Without him,
there would be no Beatles."

Opposite: Elvis Presley behind the wheel
of a Cadillac convertible in 1956, the last
year in which he was truly able to venture
out in public. By the time "The King" met
the Beatles in his Hollywood mansion
in August of 1965, he was a virtual
prisoner of his own fame, and John
was disappointed with the superficial
reality of his one-time idol.

Grabbing hold of old exercise books, he would fill them with cartoons, nonsense verse, and outrageous caricatures of the teachers. The cover of each book would bear the title *The Daily Howl,* and these would then be passed around, under the desks, to the delight of his schoolmates (and, quite often, the teachers, as well).

The poems, which usually contained more rhyme than reason, displayed a love for wordplay that John would later put to good use in classic songs such as "I Am The Walrus." By switching letters, replacing them, or omitting them completely, John could not only make words sound different, but sometimes imbue them with a double meaning. So it was that the then-popular Davy Crockett was lampooned in *The Story of Davy Crutch-Head,* while other little gems included *Tales of Hermit Fred* and *The Land of the Lunapots,* as well as a weather report stating that "Tomorrow will be Muggy . . . followed by Tuggy, Wuggy and Thuggy."

Until now, these compositions were one of the very few outlets for John to express his individuality, to mark himself out as different from the rest. Little did he realize that just around the corner an event was about to take place that would totally reshape the face of Western popular culture, and, along with it, his own life as well as those of millions of others. It would hit with the impact of an earthquake, the tremors of which are being felt to this day.

Popular (and therefore white) songs of the early 1950s were invariably pleasant, a smooth voice crooning about the joys and heartaches of love, urging people to dance, or asking "How Much Is That Doggie In The Window?" Then, on May 11, 1956, a record entitled "Heartbreak Hotel" entered the British charts. The song was performed by an unknown 21-year-old singer out of Memphis, Tennessee – Elvis Presley. The song's theme – about the feelings of loneliness following the breakup of a relationship – was nothing new in itself, but the morbid lyrics, harsh instrumental sound, and creepy atmosphere were something else entirely.

JOHN LENNON

James Dean, the pre-Elvis symbol of teen rebellion, in the famous switchblade scene from the 1955 film, *Rebel Without a Cause*. Part of John's youthful rebelliousness doubtlessly came from Dean's influence.

Clearly, since his "baby" left him, the singer had been suffering from a near-suicidal case of the blues, and he was now inviting the listener to join him in his misery and self-pity. His voice was both sensual and threatening, and the echo that it was buried in gave the impression that he was delivering his message from the farthest corner of some melancholy, deserted town.

Hearing this performance for the first time, late at night on Radio Luxembourg, was almost like a call to arms for John. Luxembourg, the British teenage alternative to the BBC, continually broadcast the new pop songs as opposed to the lighter music that parents preferred. Listening to the sounds of Bill Haley, the Platters, and the Drifters had provided John with a pleasant-enough diversion, but now here was this mysterious stranger from across the water, talking to John about the loneliness that they both shared. It was a subject that he understood, and the language appealed to him.

His reaction was immediate: He had to find out more about this Elvis character. Soon, photos in British magazines and movie newsreels confirmed the unlikely rumors he'd been hearing: The man with the raw, bluesy voice was, in fact, white. Even more surprising was his actual appearance, which was anything but conventional. His top lip seemed to be fixed in a permanent sneer, his eyes were circled by heavy lids and dark shadows, and his long hair was greased back in a style similar to that of movie star Tony Curtis. Similar, but not identical. Curtis was clean-cut; Elvis wore sideburns, that vaguely threatening trademark of the sullen lower classes. He looked odd, all right. He even had an odd name!

"Nothing really affected me until Elvis," John later reflected, and this simple statement just about says it all. At that moment the effect upon him was total, almost as if everything that had happened to him until then didn't matter. Sure, John had been impressed by James Dean in *Rebel Without a Cause,* and by the spectacle of the classroom violence instigated by the menacing young Vic Morrow in *The Blackboard Jungle,* but that was only acting. Elvis, on the other hand, was the living reality.

John acted quickly. Out went the old clothes and the conventional image, to be replaced by an Elvis hairstyle, Elvis sideburns, extra-tight jeans – called "drainpipes" – and crepe-soled shoes. He has turned himself into a full-fledged Teddy boy, so called in Britain because of the long, Edwardian-style drape coats that the rock 'n' rollers wore. As such, he now had the perfect excuse for looking mean and moody; that's the way Elvis looked, and Elvis was King!

If John had been difficult to handle before, he now became almost impossible, at home as well as at school. Mimi noticed a change in his behavior right away, especially in terms of his untidiness.

Ray Coleman's *John Winston Lennon* quotes Mimi as recalling, "He became a mess, almost overnight, and all because of Elvis Presley, I say. He had a poster of him in his bedroom. There was a pajama top in the bathroom, the trousers in the bedroom, socks somewhere else, shirts flung on the floor. . . . What he wouldn't come to terms with was that I had a house to run. Oh, he was a mess and a problem in those years. Elvis Presley!"

As things turned out, the next few years were ones of constant battles between aunt and nephew. "There's going to be a change in this house," she would shout at him. "We're going to have law and order!"

Not that Mimi's warnings had much effect. John was now heavily into rock 'n' roll, and little else mattered. "It was the only thing to get through to me after all the things that were happening when I was 15," he said many years later to *Rolling Stone* interviewer Jann Wenner. "Rock and roll was real, everything else was unreal. And the thing about rock and roll, good rock and roll – whatever good means – is that it's real, and realism gets through to you despite yourself. You recognize something in it which is true. . . ."

Carl Perkins, a man who made waves with his music rather than with an image. The Quarry Men regularly performed Perkins compositions, including "Blue Suede Shoes," "Tennessee," and "Your True Love." Later, the Beatles would record cover versions of "Matchbox," "Honey Don't," and "Everybody's Trying To Be My Baby."

JOHN LENNON

Lonnie Donegan, the "King of Skiffle," who illustrated to John Lennon and other
British youngsters that the creation of soul-stirring music
was within everybody's grasp.

JOHN LENNON

The skiffle sound, Liverpool-style. This is the first photograph of John Lennon
and Paul McCartney together, playing with the Quarry Men at the
New Clubmoor Hall on November 23, 1957.

The emergence of Elvis had been only the beginning, and within a very short space of time John, like most other British teenagers, was also listening to the sounds of the Americans Little Richard, Chuck Berry, Jerry Lee Lewis, Carl Perkins . . . and a Britisher named Lonnie Donegan.

In Britain, Donegan was the man who brought a new form of popular music to the masses. When his 1954 cover version of the old Huddie "Leadbelly" Ledbetter song, "Rock Island Line," suddenly became a hit in January of 1956, it started a craze among teenagers for his particular brand of music, called "skiffle." A crude blending of folk, jazz, and blues, it was not so much the quality of the skiffle sound that caused a sensation, but more the ease with which that sound was produced.

The Lonnie Donegan Skiffle Group featured drums, upright double bass, and two guitarists. Donegan took the lead, playing a basic three-chord style, and performed the whining, nasal-sounding vocals. In 1956 and '57 he enjoyed a succession of hits with "Putting On The Style," "Cumberland Gap," and "Don't You Rock Me Daddy-O." Donegan later charted in America with "Does Your Chewing Gum Lose Its Flavor (On the Bedpost Overnight.)" The less-than-sophisticated skiffle sound was cheap and easy to duplicate, and within a short space of time thousands of skiffle groups sprang up all over Britain.

The most difficult and expensive instrument to acquire was the double bass, and so for this the kids improvised. A broom handle would be poked through a hole in an upturned tea-chest, and a length of cord then run between the two, producing an instant "tea-chest bass." Percussive rhythm, on the other hand, would be provided by someone strumming thimbled fingers up and down on an old washboard.

This was it – do-it-yourself rock 'n' roll! John wouldn't even bother dreaming about trying to match the god-like Elvis, but here was something that was well within his grasp. Now, all he had to do was persuade either Mimi or Julia to buy him a guitar; no easy task. Mimi, of course, was dead set against any ideas he might have of imitating the "vulgar" Presley, and Julia didn't want to undermine her sister's authority.

Another view of the first public performance of the Quarry Men. Because local
thugs thought it would be fun to beat up "loudmouthed Lennon," the band
ducked out of sight as soon as this performance was over.

JOHN LENNON

The solution was for John himself to send off for an ultra-cheap mail-order guitar – "guaranteed not to split" – and have it posted to Julia's address. The following year, 1957, Mimi would relent, and buy him a better guitar just so that he would "get it out of his system." In Philip Norman's *Shout! The Beatles in Their Generation,* Mimi remembers that she'd send John outside the front door to practice: "He stood there leaning against the wall so long," she recalled, "I think he wore some of the brickwork away with his behind."

Julia, who could play the banjo, set about teaching her son some of the chords that she knew, and soon the aspiring star was belting out his version of "Rock Island Line" and searching around for fellow musicians to form a band.

He didn't have to look far. At school, Rod Davis had recently purchased a banjo, while Eric Griffiths already had a guitar and knew Colin Hanton, an apprentice upholsterer with a new drum kit. Other friends, such as Bill Smith, Nigel Whalley, Ivan Vaughan, and Len Garry, alternated on tea-chest bass, and the washboard was taken up by none other than Pete Shotton.

After initially naming the group the Blackjacks, John then settled on the Quarry Men, in surprising reference to Quarry Bank Grammar and a line in the school song, "Quarry men strong before our birth." John made all of the decisions, of course, being the group's undisputed leader, dictating the songs that they perform – solid rock 'n' roll favorites, such as "Let's Have A Party" – and taking care of all the lead vocals.

The group's first rehearsal took place at Eric Griffiths's house. So far, so good, but their first audition – in which they failed to qualify for a TV talent contest – was a dismal failure, and their first public performance was on the back of a coal truck, at a carnival in Rosebery Street, Liverpool, on June 22, 1957.

Not the most auspicious of beginnings. Regardless, other modest engagements were secured, and for the most part the ever-reliable Julia allowed rehearsals to take place at her home. She would tune Rod Davis's banjo and John's guitar similarly, with the result that John would play banjo chords using just the top four strings of his guitar. It was this peculiar style that

Quarry Men Paul McCartney (playing a right-handed guitar upside-down), Ken Brown, and John, at the Casbah Coffee Club in Liverpool.

Bespectacled Buddy Holly, with the Crickets, Jerry Allison (top) and Joe B. Mauldin (bottom). Holly's music influenced John tremendously.

JOHN LENNON

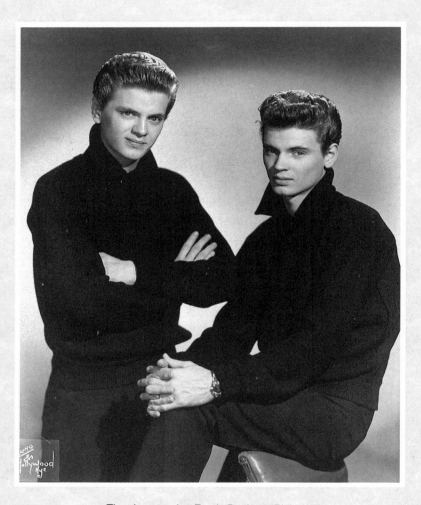

The chart-topping Everly Brothers, Phil and Don, whose tight vocal harmonies heavily influenced John Lennon and Paul McCartney during the late fifties and very early sixties.

initially gained the attention of 15-year-old Paul McCartney, when he saw John for the first time at a garden fete, in the field behind St. Peter's Church in Woolton, on July 6, 1957.

Paul, who had been brought to see the Quarry Men by mutual friend Ivan Vaughan, was not only fascinated by the Teddy boy's flashy checked shirt, his strange method of playing, and his adlibbed lyrics, but also by the way in which he peered menacingly at the audience. John, in fact, had trouble *seeing* the audience; extremely nearsighted from an early age, he was reluctant to wear glasses in public. (Later, photos of bespectacled rock star Buddy Holly at least partially convinced him otherwise.)

Afterwards, while the Quarry Men were setting up their equipment for the evening dance in the church hall, Ivan introduced Paul to the band members. "John said 'hello,' but as usual he was very withdrawn," recalls Pete Shotton. "He was always very suspicious of other people and wanted to make them come to him. He wasn't always outgoing as a kid, but after a few minutes of standing awkwardly and saying virtually nothing, Paul, being the exuberant type of person that he was, got his guitar out and started playing, and then he and John had this thing in common."

McCartney, in fact, managed to impress John and the rest of the group right away, by playing Eddie Cochran's "Twenty Flight Rock" and Gene Vincent's "Be-Bop-A-Lula," writing down the correct lyrics to these two numbers, and then tuning the guitars of both John and Eric Griffiths. John, for his part, could never memorize the words to songs – the first one that he learned properly was Buddy Holly's "That'll Be The Day" – and he couldn't tune a guitar. Paul's abilities in these areas were helpful – what's more, the new kid even looked a bit like Elvis!

"Later, John and I walked home alone," Shotton remembers, "and John said to me, 'What do you think of him?' I said 'I like him,' and he said, 'What about asking him to join the band then?' So I said 'Well, if he wants to, it's okay with me.' Okay with me! Lucky you, Paul!"

"I had a group, I was the singer and the leader," John recounted to Jann Wenner in an interview with *Rolling Stone* in 1970. "I met Paul and I made a decision whether to – and he made a decision, too – have him in the group: Was it better to have a guy who was better than the people I had in, obviously, or not? To make the group stronger or let me be stronger? That decision was to let Paul in and make the group stronger."

For Pete Shotton and John's other friends, playing in the band was just an enjoyable pastime. For John it was turning into a serious business. Hunter Davies's *The Beatles: The Authorized Biography* reports John's assertion that, "That was the day, the day that I met Paul, that it started moving."

For the first time John had a goal, some form of ambition, but in the meantime what was he going to do in order to keep the adults off his back?

Writer Philip Norman, author of *Shout!,* notes that John later recalled, "I was just drifting. I wouldn't study at school, and when I was put in for nine GCEs I was a hopeless failure."

The GCEs were the certificates required in each subject at the age of 16, in order for the student to move on to higher education. Five passes were needed, and in John's case none were achieved. For Mimi, this spelled complete disaster, but the fact that John had failed every subject by just one grade demonstrated to his principal, Mr. Pobjoy, that he had the ability. All he needed to do was put forth the proper effort. For this reason, Pobjoy put in a good report for the wayward student, helping him to enter Liverpool College of Art. This was a prospect that even John, for once, was looking forward to. Now he would just have to apply himself more seriously.

"I was disappointed at not getting art at GCE," he admitted later to biographer Hunter Davies, "but I'd given up. All they were interested in was neatness. I was never neat. I used to mix all the colors together. We had one question which said do a picture of 'travel.' I drew a picture of a hunchback, with warts all over him. They obviously didn't dig that."

John Lennon's individualistic pursuit of the arts had begun.

Eddie Cochran was one of the first-generation American rock 'n' rollers who toured Britain. Musically skilled, energetic, and in constant motion, he exemplified the standard of showmanship that John aspired to. It was while in the U.K. in 1960 that Cochran was killed in a car crash en route to an airport; rocker Gene Vincent was badly injured in the same accident.

John's Aunt Mimi, shown here in a 1964 photograph, was frequently at odds with her rebellious nephew during his adolescence. Still, her support of him was essentially unwavering, and helped him to survive his art school debacle and early musical disappointments.

CHAPTER 3

ART SCHOOL DROPOUT

*"I should have been an
illustrator or in the painting
school, but I found myself
in lettering . . . They might
as well have put me in
sky-diving. . . ."*

JOHN LENNON
1968
(*The Beatles: The Authorized Biography* by Hunter Davies)

Liverpool College of Art, where John spent most of his time either disrupting
classes or rehearsing with his band . . . when he bothered to show up at all.

Approaching his 17th birthday, John had, until now, led a fairly conventional existence. Yes, his very early life had been rocky, but since the age of five he had been brought up in an atmosphere of love and stability, and the joys and setbacks he had experienced were not really unusual.

Now, however, he was about to embark on a life-long journey that would take in an incredible number of landmark events. Prior to the end of his time at Quarry Bank nothing remarkable had happened to him, but after his departure for Art College it was as if everything intensified and accelerated. Over the next 23 years, incidents of great significance would pile one on top of the other, and there would be a constant flow of people passing through his life; enough, indeed, to fill *several* lifetimes.

Yet all of this would have sounded totally ridiculous, both to John and to everyone who knew him, when he turned up for his interview at Liverpool College of Art in the fall of 1957. Wearing Uncle George's old brown jacket, plus shirt and tie, with an eye-catching portfolio of his Quarry Bank work under his arm and Aunt Mimi in tow, he gained entry and took what appeared to be his last chance for a secure future. His school days having been a complete write-off, he was lucky to get this opportunity. Now, he had better do some work, otherwise . . . well, Mimi shuddered to think.

The College was situated in Liverpool's bohemian neighborhood near the city center, an area populated by sculptors, painters, writers, and poets. In line with this, the students were typical arty types; young intellectuals, whose favorite music was the traditional ("trad") jazz that they listened to at local cellar clubs such as The Cavern. Smooth in appearance as well as mannerisms, their typical dress would be casual coats, chunky sweaters, and suede shoes.

The Liverpool Institute, the high school attended by both Paul and George, and situated next door to the Liverpool College of Art (visible at left).

Then along came Lennon, a vision with greased back hair, long sideburns, pale blue Edwardian jacket, black "drainpipes," lilac shirt, bootlace tie, and crepe-soled shoes. Needless to say, eyes rolled and heads turned when this character showed up for registration.

This was not, however, the reaction of Bill Harry, an ambitious, down-to-earth Liverpudlian who had enrolled at the college a year before. Always drawn to originality, both in life as well as in art, Bill felt that he had little in common with his conventional fellow students, and so when he first noticed John sitting in the canteen – he could hardly miss him – he regarded him as a welcome change.

"You have to remember that in those days things were very, very strict," says Bill, "not only in the way that people looked but also in terms of their behavior. They had more respect for their 'superiors,' they did what they were told, they conformed a hell of a lot more. Rock 'n' roll would bring a lot of freedom to young people, but it hadn't done so yet; there wasn't really a rock culture or, for that matter, a youth culture. So word about John soon spread around the college.

"I was already writing for music magazines, and so being heavily into writing, reading and other forms of art, I tended to seek out creative people who I thought I could get on with. After I saw John we soon started talking, and we'd go for drinks at Ye Cracke [a pub near the college] and to friends' places in the evenings."

So far, so good. But while he had been looking forward to the opportunity to concentrate on the kind of drawing that he enjoyed doing, and to express himself with the paintbrush, John soon found out that he would instead be attending classes dealing in geometry, architecture, object drawing, and lettering. This was just like being at school!

JOHN LENNON

Ye Cracke, a pub located around the corner from the Art College; John and his
cronies frequently held court here.

To make matters worse, he had to put up with strict, narrow-minded instructors who clearly didn't have a clue what he was about, and a bunch of stuck-up college kids who got on his nerves. His response, as usual, was swift. Determined to ignore the established rules and regulations, he decided to enjoy himself in his own sweet way – disrupting the classes when he bothered to attend, and drinking with new friends such as Geoff Mohammed and Tony Carricker, when he chose to go absent. In no time at all, John had managed to land himself with the same dubious reputation that he had earned at Quarry Bank.

Imagine the scene: For the weekly "life" class, 15 students would be quietly standing behind their easels in Room 71, sketching the body of 27-year-old nude model June Furlong. Having walked around and passed comment on the various illustrations, the teacher would then leave for a while, at which point John would let out a little snigger from the back of the room. Nobody would take any notice of this, but shortly afterwards he would make a similar but slightly louder noise. Again, everyone would try to get on with his or her work, and a minute or so would pass before the serious mood would be interrupted by another, more exaggerated giggle, followed shortly thereafter by John's full-scale hysterical shriek. By now, everybody, including the naked model, would be convulsed with laughter, and John would then follow this up by jumping into her lap and necking with her.

The offbeat side of John's nature also became apparent at the end of another life class session, when the afternoon's work was handed in. Whereas the other students had produced straightforward drawings of June, the portrait that John came up with was of the only item that she was wearing; her wristwatch. Highly original, but it didn't amuse the teacher.

Soon, relations between John and his instructors had deteriorated to such an extent that he actively went out of his way to annoy them. Mimi recalled waking up at 3 o'clock one morning and going downstairs to see him painting furiously, preparing work that had to be handed in within a few hours. She sat there in the living room, watching him finish his masterpiece and then smother it with salt, pepper, and sugar that he had fetched from the kitchen. Writer George Tremlett's *The John Lennon Story* reports what happened next:

"What on earth are you doing?" Mimi demanded. "You'll get thrown out of college."

"Look," said John, referring to one of the teachers, "he hates me, and I'm not very fond of him!"

Mimi couldn't believe this act of willful provocation, and when he was about to leave for class, she and John engaged in a tug-of-war over the painting in the driveway. No need to say who won, except that the nephew returned later that day, smiling triumphantly. "He never said a thing," commented John about the lecturer. "He just looked at it and walked away, but he knew why I had done it, all right. He knew!"

Meanwhile, with matters running less than smoothly at college, John's musical ambitions weren't exactly going to plan, either. After recruiting the services of Paul McCartney, the Quarry Men had managed to play at various small clubs around Liverpool during the last few months of 1957 and the first part of 1958. Then the bookings dried up, and for several months the group was reduced to playing at private parties.

From the outset of his art school career, John felt stifled by the conservative, "proper" curriculum. Against the wishes of his instructors, then, he developed his penchant for drawing misshapen, satirical figures. This amusing example was selected for the cover of a program for a 1964 charity revue, *The Night of a Hundred Stars*.

JOHN LENNON

Left: Fifteen-year-old George Harrison at around the time that the unruly influence of John Lennon began making an impact on his life. Aunt Mimi, who was not immediately impressed by George, tried to discourage John from associating with "that working class lad" who wore flashy clothes.

Opposite: 1 Blomfield Road, the Liverpool house that Julia Lennon shared with her boyfriend, "Twitchy," and where John and Paul rehearsed their music in the bathroom. It was here that John was informed by a policeman that his mother had been killed.

Some of the band members lost interest and quit, but by this time 15-year-old George Harrison had joined the line-up.

In John's eyes George was just a kid, but the way that he played tunes like "Raunchy" and "Guitar Boogie" was certainly impressive, and besides, his mother was an easygoing woman who allowed the group to practice in the Harrison home. With benefits such as these to offer, George was in. John had, unwittingly, put together the nucleus of the Beatles.

George was, in fact, a schoolmate of Paul's, attending the Liverpool Institute with him. By happy coincidence, this school was situated immediately next door to the Liverpool College of Art, and so most lunchtimes Lennon, McCartney, and Harrison would get together for a practice session in either the canteen or Room 21 of the college, entertaining the students with renditions of songs by the likes of Little Richard, Buddy Holly, and the Everly Brothers.

Just about the only family members giving their full support to these musical activities were George's parents and the ever-helpful Julia. John was still spending a lot of his free time with his mother, getting the kind of encouragement

from her that Mimi would refuse to give. Then, on the evening of July 15, 1958, disaster struck. Having spent the day at her sister's house, Julia waved goodbye and began to cross the road in order to catch the bus home. She never made it. She was hit by a car being driven by an off-duty policeman and died instantly, aged 44.

John was sitting with Julia's boyfriend, Twitchy, waiting for her to return, when a policeman knocked on the door. "It was just like it's supposed to be, the way it is in the films," he told biographer Hunter Davies a decade later. "Asking if I was her son, and all that. Then he told us, and we both went white.

"It was the worst thing that ever happened to me. We'd caught up so much, me and Julia, in just a few years. We could communicate. We got on. She was great. I thought . . . I've no responsibilities to anyone now."

Indeed, it was with this kind of attitude that John became more rebellious than ever, and turned to drink in order to blank out the pain of living in the real world. At the same time, his friends began to notice his humor sometimes taking on an even stranger edge.

According to Hunter Davies's *The Beatles,* college girlfriend Thelma Pickles remembered that, "[John] used to do a lot of cruel drawings. The day the Pope died, he did lots of drawings of him looking really awful. He did one of the Pope standing outside some big pillars outside Heaven, shaking the gates and trying to get in. Underneath it said, 'But I'm the Pope, I tell you!'"

A friend of John, Nigel Whalley, was the last person to see Julia Lennon alive, saying a few words to her on his way to Mimi's house, before walking on, hearing the screech of brakes, and turning to see a body flying through the air. In an interview which he gave several years later, Whalley recalled an evening not long after the accident when John invited him and a few other friends to Julia's old house.

"A number of us went, and we all sat down round a circular table. John said we were going to hold a seance, switched the lights down low and spread the letter cards round the table. Then he began to rotate his hand round the top of a tumbler, and it started to move and spell out words. We sat there terrified, but he seemed quite calm, almost unmoved,

Cynthia: When the "posh Miss Powell" embarked on a relationship with Lennon the Teddy boy in 1958, little could she have realized how her decision would forever change the course of her life.

and to this day I don't know whether there was a spirit there that night or if he was just having us on."

Either way, John would never quite get over the emotional stress caused by losing his mother. "I lost her twice," he asserted just before his own death. "Once as a five-year-old when I was moved in with my auntie. And once again . . . when she actually, physically died. . . . And that was really a hard time for me. It just absolutely made me very, very bitter. The underlying chip on my shoulder that I had as a youth got really big then. Being a teenager and a rock 'n' roller and an art student and my mother being killed, just when I was re-establishing a relationship with her . . . it was very traumatic for me."

"Devastating" would be another way of putting it. Having been deserted by his father and then forced to suffer the loss of his uncle, John had now been deprived of his mother, the one person who really seemed to understand him. Hurt and full of rage, he desperately needed someone to turn to, someone who could understand his inner torment, tolerate his moods, and always be there for him. That person turned out to be Cynthia Powell.

For most of the first year at the Liverpool College of Art, Cynthia had been keeping an eye on John from across the room that they both sat in, during the weekly lettering classes. Having watched his crazy antics and laughed at his outrageous jokes, she soon found herself hopelessly drawn to this unruly Teddy boy. He, on the other hand, hardly seemed to notice her, but in time this would change, for if there was ever a case of opposites attracting, then this was it.

As signified by her gentler, more refined accent, Cynthia did not live in Liverpool itself, but in Hoylake, a very respectable middle-class area situated on the Wirral, on the other side of the River Mersey. She was a shy, well-mannered girl, conscientious and hard-working. Her appearance ensured that she merged quietly into the background: modest tweed skirt and short, permed hair. As she herself observed in her 1978 book, *A Twist of Lennon,* "The only thing that John and I had in common was that we were both as blind as bats without our glasses. . . . He lived in a different world to me."

At first, John's only recognition of her came in the form of mocking the "posh" way in which "Miss Powell" spoke. He began to take more notice, however, when she allowed her hair to grow long and straight, and then dyed it blonde, making her more closely resemble the woman of his dreams, French film star Brigitte Bardot. Cynthia, for her part, was initially just amused by John's wild and often hilarious behavior, but within no time her interest turned into infatuation.

Needless to say, this was totally against the best advice of her friends, who saw her as less than well suited to that loudmouthed layabout, Lennon. His friends weren't too enthusiastic either; what did he see in that cool, snooty career girl from over the water?

Yet in spite of everyone's better judgment, the two finally broke the ice at a college party in the summer of 1958, just before the end of the academic year. They danced together and Cynthia was in seventh heaven, but when John asked her out her panicky response was to blurt out, "I'm awfully sorry, I'm engaged to this fellow in Hoylake." John snapped back, "I didn't ask you to marry me, did I?"

Having got these pleasantries out of the way, Cynthia allowed fate to take over, and she and her girlfriend joined John and his cronies at the local pub. Several drinks later, the two girls found themselves sitting alone at a table while the guys stood and talked at the bar. Cynthia, sensing that the whole episode had just been a cheap joke at her expense, decided to make a swift and silent exit. Just as she reached for the door, however, she could hear John's gravelly voice boom out above the noise of the crowd, "Didn't you know Miss Powell was a nun, then?"

"I was dragged back into focus and persuaded to stay," she recalled in her book. "How could I resist?" Well, she didn't, and for all of the highs and lows that she was to experience as a result of this momentous decision, it was one that she has never regretted.

Young Paul McCartney. Even after the start-up of John's romance with Cynthia, Paul—and music—remained dominant in John's life.

CHAPTER 4

TOO MUCH MONKEY BUSINESS

"The guitar's alright as a hobby, John, but you'll never make a living out of it."

Aunt Mimi

c. 1958

Opposite: George Harrison, Stuart Sutcliffe, and John in Hamburg, West Germany, 1960. John's experience in Hamburg was invaluable because the tough audiences demanded tight musicianship and forced John to adopt an aggressive, engaging stage presence. More important, John was able to immerse himself in a new world, one that was quite different from Liverpool. He was growing up fast.

Billy Fury, a "British Elvis" of the very early 1960s, came from the Beatles' hometown of Liverpool. On May 10, 1960, the band did, in fact, audition to be Fury's backing group, but they were rejected because of Stu Sutcliffe's poor bass playing.

As his emotional life was in turmoil, one of the few things that John had left to cling to was his music. It was becoming increasingly apparent that he was simply wasting his own and everyone else's time at art college, and that he had neither the qualifications nor the application to hold down a job that would provide him with financial security. Making music was what he enjoyed most, and it was now beginning to dawn on him that this would probably be his only route to some sort of success.

Paul McCartney, for his part, also appeared to be taken in by this idea. An academically bright boy who had, until now, always excelled at school, he too began "sagging off" (cutting class). This was not only in order to make lunchtime rehearsal sessions at the art college, but also so that he and John could go back to the McCartney home in Allerton. There, during the afternoons while Paul's father was out, the pair indulged in their favorite pastimes: songwriting and discussing girls.

Musically, Paul was easily the more accomplished of the two, capable of playing more instruments and writing songs of his own. John, on the other hand, was the original. Whereas other British performers at the time – including Paul – tended to imitate many of the characteristics of their favorite American artists, often singing with a pseudo-American accent, John's approach was all his. His strong, raw voice was made for rock 'n' roll, and while he utilized some of the vocal mannerisms of Buddy Holly, his pronunciation was clearly English. He wasn't interested in sounding like other people, but just in being himself. The way in which he ripped his way through songs was true to his character; no frills, no nonsense.

Although John had the greater talent for lyrics and Paul had a broader musical range, there were no strict ground rules in their collaboration. During the first years of their partnership, they would often work together when writing words and tunes, and although in some cases one or the other person had contributed far more to a particular song, they agreed early on to always share the credit. Although by 1964 they were rarely composing side by side, "Lennon-McCartney"

Cliff Richard, Britain's "answer" to Elvis in the late fifties. Although he never
sustained major success in the U.S., he continues to be something of a
superstar in his homeland. It was, however, Richard's brand of stylized pop
music that the Beatles rebelled against in the early sixties.

continued to appear under each title until the Beatles split in 1969. Regardless, the identity of the person singing the lead vocal provided an easy clue as to who originated each song.

Among John's first compositions were "Winston's Walk," which was never recorded; "Hello Little Girl," which was later recorded by the Fourmost; and "The One After 909," which was recorded by the Beatles in 1963 (unreleased) and 1969 (released on the *Let It Be* album). His lyrics at first tended to be of the "blue moon in June" variety – simple love poems that rhymed neatly. But as his confidence grew and he began to experiment more, the word structures became more intricate and the subject matter less familiar.

Soon a noticeable difference of style emerged between the two young composers: Whereas Paul tended to construct little stories, John concentrated on writing in the first person and expressing his own emotions. It was John who was experiencing the joys or pains of love, and who would use his songwriting to relate, much later on, his political views, his experiments with drugs, and numerous other incidents that took place in his life. And while Paul's songs were usually upbeat and optimistic, John's could often be probing and cynical.

"I was always like that, you know," he asserted during his 1980 interview with *Playboy*'s David Sheff. "I was like that before the Beatles and after the Beatles. I always asked why people did things and why society was like it was. I didn't just accept it for what it was apparently doing. I always looked below the surface."

Whereas in America during the 1950s artists such as Chuck Berry, Little Richard, Sam Cooke, and Buddy Holly wrote a lot of the material that they performed, the situation was not the

JOHN LENNON

same in Britain. There, the stars of the day usually recorded either songs that had been penned by specialist composers, or "cover" versions of American hits. It was, therefore, highly unusual for two English schoolboys to be compiling their own catalogue of songs which they, themselves, could perform. Furthermore, they didn't produce simple carbon copies of the sounds that they heard from across the Atlantic. Instead, they assimilated various American melodic styles and rhythms and put their own beat-oriented slant on them.

To the by-now 16-year-old Paul McCartney, John was someone to secretly admire; a hard-rocking Teddy boy, two years his elder, and a potentially dangerous influence who (as Paul's father had warned him) could get him "into trouble." Naturally, Paul was eager to hang out with a guy like this!

To John, on the other hand, Paul was a baby-faced, wide-eyed smoothie, who was gracious and hard working. On the surface, not his type at all, but John was nothing if not sharp. He immediately recognized that Paul's qualities could be extremely beneficial, both to him and to his group. Paul's musical talent would be of great value, his will to succeed would inspire John to write and the band to improve, and his pretty looks would charm the girls.

So, as he had done before, John had teamed up with someone who was not much like him, but who complemented him perfectly. Well aware of what he needed and what he himself had to offer, he formed his closest relationships with people who could both play on his strengths and make up for his weaknesses. This was the case with Paul, Cynthia and, just as remarkably, Stuart Sutcliffe, a small, shy, Scottish-born artist whose incredible talent had taken the college by storm.

Sutcliffe's introvert personality, vulnerable on the surface but extremely strong underneath, contrasted greatly with the extrovert John, who was always able to attract a crowd around him, and whose hard outer appearance concealed a soft center. Both had very sharp minds, however, and they saw qualities in each other that they respected and desired.

John's mean and moody appearance was largely a pose,

John, through the lens of Astrid Kirchherr, at around the time of his 20th birthday in October 1960. For a band of relative unknowns, the Beatles were fortunate to have had so many artistic portraits taken of them. But then, even early on their image and personalities attracted photographers' attention.

Opposite: The founder, the leader, and the soul of the Beatles, standing in a Hamburg doorway in the spring of 1961. No photo better captures the image John wished to convey; fourteen years later, he would choose it for the cover of his *Rock 'n' Roll* album.

JOHN LENNON

Giving it all they've got, on stage at The Cavern Club, 1961.

used for specific effect, but with Stuart it was natural. He didn't need to do much to attract the girls; his looks saw to that, as did an artistic ability which had the college instructors predicting future greatness. The fact that he led a bohemian lifestyle – living in a run-down room with a shared toilet in a large Georgian house – only added to the air of mystique around him, and to John's fascination.

This was the heyday of the "beat generation," of unorthodox young poets such as Allen Ginsberg and Jack Kerouac, and of the beatniks who read their works and spent long hours analyzing them. Unlike the traditional rhymes, these writings dealt with stream-of-consciousness, whereby the poets put the various unrelated thoughts that came tumbling out of their heads straight onto paper in verse form. John, whose own love for wordplay was as strong as ever, was absorbed by

all this. He and Stuart, together with college friends Bill Harry and Rod Murray, would stay up late into the night, drinking and talking about the new poetry.

Inspired by these sessions, as well as the thought of spending more time with Cynthia and less with Mimi, John duly informed his aunt that he was moving out of her house and into Stuart's place in Gambier Terrace, situated conveniently around the corner from the college. In a later interview with author George Tremlett, Mimi recalled John telling her, "I feel like a baby living at home," before tactfully adding, "Anyhow, I can't stand your food!" This was all that Mimi needed to hear. She let John pack his bags and gave him his full college grant money. For now, the Teddy boy would become a beatnik.

Within four weeks, however, all the money that was supposed to last him three months had been spent, and the flat that he

George, John, Paul, and Pete play on . . . for 18 people who turned out to see
them at the Palais Ballroom in Aldershot, southern England, on December 9, 1961.

was sharing with Stu and Rod Murray was in complete chaos, with clothes, paints, and garbage spread all over the floor around the mattresses that were being used in lieu of beds. By the middle of winter it was so cold, and they were all so broke, that, so the legend goes, they were reduced to burning in the middle of the room what furniture they had in order to keep warm.

Having left Mimi's in a mood of supreme confidence, boasting that he would be surviving quite happily on a diet of Chinese takeout food – "bamboo shoots and things" – John suddenly reappeared at her house with his tail firmly between his legs. Too proud to admit, however, that things hadn't gone exactly to plan, he tried to give the impression that this was just a friendly visit, and asked casually "Don't I get a cup of tea, then?" Mimi went along with his little act, and quietly

continued cooking the dinner that she was preparing for herself. This was just too much! Not having eaten for days, John couldn't resist the smell of steak and mushrooms that was wafting above his head, and so he suddenly burst into the kitchen and shouted at her: "I'll have you know, woman, I'm starving!"

Mimi gave him dinner and allowed him to stay the night. The next morning, with extra money from her in his pocket, John set off once again for the mayhem of Gambier Terrace and further adventure.

As his art studies went from bad to worse, so he became more ambitious for his band, and through the first half of 1960, thanks largely to the efforts of local businessman Allan Williams, more and more engagements – including a tour of Scotland, backing singer Johnny Gentle – were being secured.

JOHN LENNON

Drummer Pete Best (*far left*) joined the Beatles in August of 1960.
Good-looking and eager to please, he would nonetheless be dismissed from
the group just two years later.

By this time, Stu Sutcliffe had joined the group, persuaded by John to spend the then-enormous sum of £65 that he had earned from one of his paintings on a brand new bass guitar. The fact that he had no idea how to play the instrument was irrelevant; he was John's friend, John wanted him in the group, and that was that. Stu duly reciprocated by coming up with the name of the "Beatals" as a replacement for the outdated Quarry Men. Over the next few months the name would change to the Silver Beats, the Silver Beetles, the Silver Beatles and, by the middle of August 1960, the Beatles.

This same month, Pete Best was recruited as drummer, the first to fill the post on a permanent basis since Colin Hanton had quit the group the previous year. So it was that the first proper Beatles lineup featured John, Paul, and George on guitars, Stu on bass, and Pete on drums when the band turned up for a two-month stint at the newly opened Indra Club in Hamburg, West Germany, on August 17, 1960.

John by now had come to the end of his course at the Art College, after failing his lettering exams. For months, Mimi had pleaded with him to give up the guitar and concentrate on the drawing that he was good at, but the reply, according to Ray Coleman's book, *John Winston Lennon,* was always the same: "I'll be OK, I don't need the bits of paper to tell me where I'm going." Sure enough, he was heading for Hamburg and, he hoped, the big time.

Allan Williams was again responsible for setting up the booking, having already enjoyed considerable success with his placement of the far more accomplished Liverpool group, Derry and the Seniors, at The Indra's sister club, The Kaiserkeller. The Beatles would, in fact, play both venues between their late-summer arrival and November 30, and although they would have to put up with poor money, terrible

In 1963 the leader of the Pete Best All-Stars smiles valiantly and tries to rebuild
his shattered career. Five years later he would be working in a bakery.

accommodations, and very demanding hours, Hamburg would prove to be a major turning point.

The Indra and Kaiserkeller were situated on the Grosse Freiheit, in the heart of the dock city's red-light district, an area populated by pimps, prostitutes, sailors, and an assortment of others visitors in search of "a good time." Everywhere the Beatles turned they saw neon signs that pointed them in the direction of bars and strip joints, while half-naked women paraded up and down, displaying the ample goods that they had to offer. What's more, it was these kinds of people – a combination of thugs, villains, and down-and-outs – who made up a large proportion of the audiences that the Liverpool boys would have to perform to every night.

The group's stint at The Indra lasted only a few weeks before the seedy strip-palace-turned-rock-club was closed down by its owner, Bruno Koschmider, owing to lack of business and complaints about noise. The Beatles then moved to The Kaiserkeller, an altogether different proposition. Far more people packed themselves into this much larger venue, and apart from being slightly overwhelmed by all this, the band also felt lost in the middle of what seemed to be a huge stage; huge, that is, compared to anything that they had played on before.

After observing the stiffness of their stage movements – what there was of them – Allan Williams repeatedly told the inexperienced entertainers to "make a show," and he was promptly imitated by both Koschmider and the customers, who would also urge them to "mak show." For John, this was a license to go completely wild; if it was a show they wanted, then it was a show they were going to get!

Not content with simply jumping around the stage like a cross between Elvis, Little Richard, and Jerry Lee Lewis, John

The primitive rocker, on stage at
Hamburg's Top Ten Club.

decided that it would also be fun to really intimidate these
postwar Germans, and force them to swallow their already-
bruised national pride. It may have been 15 years since the
Second World War, but the ever-sensitive John wasn't prepared
to forgive his audience for the crimes that their nation had
committed, nor was he about to let them forget. Comments
such as "What did you do during the war?" and "Get back to
your tank" soon became part of his on-stage patter, and in
case anyone couldn't understand or hear him above the general
noise, he would press the point home by goose-stepping
up and down, calling them "Bloody Krauts" and shouting
"Heil Hitler!"

Needless to say, the customers were not charmed by this
sort of behavior, but still they loved the raw brand of rock 'n'
roll that they were hearing, and they would try to encourage
more of the same by sending crates of beer up onto the stage.
Mixed with pep pills supplied by the club's waiters, this helped
the Beatles endure the exhausting six-hour sessions that they
would sometimes have to play. Additionally, it gave John added
confidence with which to face his "fans"; on at least one
occasion he walked on stage wearing just a swimming costume
and a toilet seat around his neck!

Aside from all the frivolity, however, there were also many
benefits that the Beatles were gaining from their time in
Hamburg. As human beings, the incredible things that they
were seeing, hearing, and experiencing were causing them
to grow up overnight; as performers, the long hours and
demanding audiences were teaching them to play more tightly
as a band, improving their musicianship and hardening
their voices.

During this period, John's friendship with Stuart Sutcliffe
became stronger than ever. Stu met and fell in love with
Astrid Kirchherr, a 22-year-old designer and photographer
whose stunning wardrobe sense – all-black suede jacket and
leather skirt – and strong opinions on fashion, art, and music
were to have a profound effect on all of the Beatles over the
course of the next two years.

The early Beatles as proto-punks. Pete, George, John, Paul, and Stu, growing up overnight in Hamburg, October 1960.

Astrid's beautiful blonde looks naturally caught John's eye as yet another Bardot look-alike, but it was her intellect and her friendly willingness to listen to whatever he had to say that most attracted him to her. The fact that she was Stuart's girlfriend ruled out any possibility of a romantic relationship between them, but John still spent a great deal of his spare time with the couple, talking, drinking, and investigating Astrid's large collection of classical books.

"John had this knowledge of everything that surrounded him, because he had particularly high intelligence," Astrid told Ray Coleman. "But he didn't have much experience, and he was so nosey . . . I thought of him as a gentle, sentimental boy who was in such a hurry to find out about everything. Stuart was the same, but really he had a deeper natural intelligence than John. When they were together, it was very powerful for them both."

Soon, however, the first Hamburg trip ended in disarray, after the Beatles broke their contract with The Kaiserkeller by playing at the rival Top Ten Club. George, reported to the authorities for being under-age, was deported, as were Paul and Pete for supposedly setting fire to the wallpaper in their grubby living quarters. Stu decided to stay on with Astrid, and so it was a very depressed John who set out alone for the return trip to England on December 10, 1960.

Yet more than 500 hours of playing, crammed into little over three months, had left their mark, and when the Beatles appeared at the Town Hall Ballroom in Litherland, Liverpool, on December 27, they experienced the first stirrings of what would later come to be known as Beatlemania. The audience, swept away by the band's new-found magnetism, rushed forward to the front of the stage, and all at once the no-hopers had been transformed into local heroes.

The next 18 months would not be without their fair share of letdowns, but for John, who was hanging all of his hopes on the group's fortunes, there was now at least some light at the end of the tunnel.

JOHN LENNON

THE SECRET HUSBAND

"Walking about, married: It was like walking about with odd socks on or your flies open."

JOHN LENNON
1968
(*The Beatles: The Authorized Biography* by Hunter Davies)

Opposite: Sweating for success: John Lennon during a 1962 rehearsal session at The Cavern Club, the clammy, musty basement venue where the walls actually perspired. No matter, for it was at The Cavern that John's professional goals would begin to come true.

By early 1962, the Beatles had attracted a great deal of attention in the Liverpool area, and had become local favorites. Bill Harry's *Mersey Beat*—here making official the Beatles' popularity—had published some of John's writing in its early issues. Note the ad at top right for NEMS, Brian Epstein's record store, and the misspelling of Paul's surname.

Although he would join his friends on stage on a few more occasions, Stuart Sutcliffe's decision to remain with Astrid in Hamburg meant that he had effectively left the Beatles. His reasons for this were two-fold. First, he obviously wanted to spend more time with the new love of his life; and second, while it had been John who had asked him to join the band in the first place, it was also John – together with Paul – who mercilessly criticized his poor bass playing and made fun of him in public.

This kind of behavior was not unusual, for while John's rapier-like wit could make even the most mundane situations appear funny, he would also use it to devastating effect to embarrass many of those who were closest to him.

"He could destroy people with his verbal wit," asserts his former college friend, Bill Harry. "He'd do this all the time, and it surprised me the way he used to be cruel with Stuart, because I knew how close they were. He'd really put him down, and he'd put down anyone – including Cynthia – if he had the opportunity. If you were the sort of person who'd let him get away with it, he'd be quite cutting – especially after a few drinks – and that made some people frightened of him, but most of it was show.

"There again, many people also didn't catch onto his bizarre sense of humor, but in my case I loved it, I understood it. That's why I asked him to show me some of his poetry, which I'd heard about. At first, I got the impression that he was reluctant to do so, because poetry wasn't the sort of thing that a macho guy from the North [of England] would write! So when he did show me one of his poems, he was really surprised at how much I liked it."

At around this time, Bill was planning to start *Mersey Beat,* a biweekly newspaper dealing with the then-thriving rock (or "pop") music scene in the area. Each issue would contain news items, record reviews, concert listings, and feature stories about – or interviews with – the various artists in and around Liverpool. Taken by the offbeat humor of John's poetry, Bill asked him to contribute a piece to the first issue, and John

Liverpool's The Cavern Club, seen here in 1964, became synonymous with the early Beatles. Many other bands played here as well, even though it was not unknown for band members or their roadies to be mugged outside by local toughs.

responded by coming up with "Being a Short Diversion on the Dubious Origins of Beatles," a brief tale describing, in John's own irresistible style, how his group had been formed.

Bill was delighted with the article, and John was delighted with his reaction, so much so that soon afterwards he walked into the *Mersey Beat* offices and handed the editor a bundle of more than 250 cartoons, drawings, poems, and short stories – enough Lennon material to satisfy even the most impatient reader.

In the meantime, two very important events had taken place: During February and March 1961, The Beatles had started playing regularly at The Cavern Club, the venue which would become synonymous with their name in the years to come, and in May, during their second trip to Hamburg, they had made their first professional recordings.

With Bert Kaempfert producing, they backed singer Tony Sheridan on three songs, taped a Lennon-Harrison instrumental entitled "Cry For A Shadow," and performed their own rock arrangement of the old Eddie Cantor favorite, "Ain't She Sweet." John sang the lead vocal on this and, even at the age of 20, the unmistakable, raw-throated Lennon delivery was clearly shaping up.

Later in the year, two weeks before his 21st birthday, John was given a £100 cash gift by his Aunt Elizabeth in Scotland, prompting him and Paul to immediately spend the lot on a two-week vacation in Paris. While there, they hung around the various cafes, clubs, and bars, and also met with a friend of Astrid's, Jurgen Vollmer.

Jurgen was sporting a strange hairstyle, with his hair combed forward over his forehead, similar to that adopted by Stuart

JOHN LENNON

Right: A Cavern Club membership card from 1964. If the bearer hoped to use it to catch the Beatles, he or she was out of luck, for the group did not perform at the club after 1963.

By 1966, the Merseybeat scene had nose-dived and The Cavern was surrounded by derelict warehouses.

Today, Cavern Walks, a popular shopping mall, stands on the former site of the club where the Beatles appeared 274 times.

Sutcliffe when the Beatles had last seen him in Germany some months before. At that time, John had viewed this – in addition to the Astrid-inspired all-black look, complete with leather pants – as yet another opportunity to publicly put Stu down. Now, however, with persuasion from Jurgen, John and Paul decided to follow the fashion. John's Teddy boy days were finally over; he was now a "moptop."

Back in Liverpool, gigs at The Cavern were enabling him to perfect his all-round appearance as well as his banter with the audience. Here was born the famous Lennon stance: legs apart, head arched back, and guitar held up to the chest, largely a result of his extreme short-sightedness when not wearing his glasses on stage. Unable to gauge the reactions of those sitting facing him, John felt safest when projecting his well-practiced tough guy image.

The customers, of course, were mainly Liverpool locals, but they, like many of those in Hamburg, were still subjected to John's hard-bitten humor, as well as his priceless ability to turn any situation upside down on its head. The Lennon wit persevered – no matter that The Cavern was a dark, damp, musty cellar, with limited space and even more limited facilities. The wiring was hardly up to present-day safety standards (not to mention early-'60s safety standards), and with sweat quite literally dripping down the walls, it was not unusual for the musical equipment to short-circuit.

Keef Hartley, who would later be a drummer with Rory Storm and the Hurricanes, John Mayall's Bluesbreakers, and his own Keef Hartley Band, was occasionally among the kids who were crammed together, watching the Beatles perform at the club. In an interview with this author in 1981, he recalled John's method of coping with the poor conditions.

"The electrics weren't the best thing that happened at The Cavern, and either the amps would pack up or there would be a complete power cut. If this happened, John would immediately jump up onto the piano and go into this routine: 'And here we have so-and-so, who's in a string bag . . . no arms, no legs,' and he would introduce McCartney. It was completely

The Beatles backed singer Tony Sheridan on a brief set recorded in Hamburg in the spring of 1960. These recordings, raw but undeniably interesting, are widely available today.

Brian Epstein, the successful, sophisticated 27-year-old businessman with the will—if not necessarily the know-how—to take a group of unknowns to the very pinnacle of show business. Epstein may have made mistakes along the way, but it was his love for the Beatles, his ingenuity and dedication, that made everybody's dreams come true.

Opposite: Brian Epstein sits on the stage of The Cavern, the basement club where he first saw the Beatles perform on November 9, 1961. He would later title his autobiography *A Cellarful of Noise,* a book referred to sardonically by John as *A Cellarful of Boys.*

unrehearsed, but at the same time it was 'instant Lennon,' with that sick, sick humor of his! That gave the Beatles a tremendous advantage over all of the other bands, and I'm sure that people who went regularly to The Cavern were almost more entertained by that than by the live music."

While the girls were at the same time in awe of John and somewhat scared of his sharp tongue, the guys admired his manliness; he became for them something of a role model. Either way he had a magnetic presence, and one person who was immediately drawn toward this was Brian Epstein, who first saw the Beatles perform during a lunchtime session at The Cavern on November 9, 1961.

Epstein, the manager of a large record store in the center of Liverpool, was, as has been well documented, a homosexual who was helplessly attracted to John, the macho rocker who swore on stage, smoked while playing, turned his back on the audience, and stopped in the middle of a song whenever he felt like it. This was, however, by no means the only reason for Brian's interest in the group.

"I was immediately struck by their music, their beat, and their sense of humor, actually, on stage," he asserted in a 1963 BBC Television interview. "And even afterwards, when I met them, I was struck again by their personal charm, and it was there that really it all started."

Certainly it did. Epstein, a suave, sophisticated businessman who harbored frustrated showbiz ambitions, moved quickly to take the Beatles under his wing, resolving to smooth out their image, curb their lack of professionalism, and gain them a recording contract through his contacts in the record industry. During their second business meeting, while the other band members were hesitating over whether or not to take up Epstein on his offer, it was John, the leader, as decisive and straightforward as ever, who stepped forward and said, "Right then, Brian, manage us now. Where's the contract? I'll sign it."

Sure enough, after the leather gear had been discarded and the Beatles outfitted in suits, shirts, and ties, Epstein began to

JOHN LENNON

A bootleg pressing of "I'm Sure to Fall," one of the numbers recorded by the Beatles for their unsuccessful Decca Records audition on New Year's Day, 1962.

gain more prestigious local bookings for them. John, never one to conform to the rules, felt duty-bound to rebel against this restyling, and so like a naughty schoolboy he would walk around with his tie crooked and top shirt button undone. Underneath this show of defiance, however, he obviously recognized the good sense in Brian's actions, otherwise he wouldn't have put up with them.

A series of record company refusals during the first months of 1962 sorely tested the band members' faith, but Epstein delivered on his promise when, on May 9, he informed them that he had secured a recording contract with EMI's Parlophone label. The Beatles were in the middle of a seven-week season at The Star-Club in Hamburg when they received the good news, but for John this was sandwiched between some very traumatic events.

On arriving at Hamburg Airport on April 11, the Beatles were greeted by Astrid and the news that Stuart Sutcliffe had died the previous day of a suspected blood clot on the brain. He was only 21. Although they hadn't been seeing as much of each other lately as during the previous year, John and Stu had regularly kept in touch by letter. For both of them this was a form of release, a way of expressing some of their innermost thoughts, without fear of ridicule by those around them. Pages and pages would travel back and forth between England and West Germany, detailing many of the things, both good and bad, that had taken place recently, accompanied by cartoons, jokes, and poems. Hunter Davies, in his book, *The Beatles,* cites one of the most revealing pieces, in which John described to Stu his feelings of guilt over the way that he knew he sometimes hurt people:

"I can't remember anything without a sadness
So deep that it hardly becomes known to me.
So deep that its tears leave me a spectator
of my own stupidity."

In return, many of Stu's letters in recent months had described the blinding, unbearable headaches that he had been suffering from, and which doctors had failed to diagnose. The last thing that John had expected, however, was for him to die so suddenly, and his reaction was two-fold: First, echoing the situation when Uncle George had died almost five years earlier, John burst into a fit of hysterical laughter (hardly what Astrid – having arrived at the airport straight from the hospital – could have needed). Then, without shedding any public tears, he withdrew into himself and spoke very little about the subject. One of the few things he did say came in the form of this typical down-to-earth advice to Stuart's distraught girlfriend, revealed by biographer Ray Coleman in *John Winston Lennon:* "Make your decision. You either die with him or you go on living."

There it was. Cut and dried. With John there was no in-between.

"I knew that he and Stuart genuinely loved each other," Astrid recalled for Coleman. "They told me so, when they got loose. . . . How John got over that period I'll never know."

What he did, in fact, was to absorb himself in his music. He was getting pretty used to suffering tragedy by now, and his way of dealing with it was to confine it to the past and get on with the present.

More unpleasantness lay ahead, for next on the agenda was the ousting of Pete Best from his position as the Beatles' drummer. The quietest member of the group, Pete was also arguably the handsomest, and certainly the one that the girls at The Cavern most swooned over. Pete's recollection of his dismissal, reported by him in his 1985 autobiography, *Beatle! The Pete Best Story,* co-written by Patrick Doncaster, is blunt and unsentimental. In the pre-Epstein days, Pete and his mother had presided over many of the band's bookings, yet his only reward for staying faithful through thick and thin, and helping to gain the prized recording contract, was to be told by Brian that "The boys want you out and Ringo in. . . ."

Richard "Ringo Starr" Starkey was at that time a competent but unremarkable drummer playing with Rory Storm and the Hurricanes, someone who had become friendly with the

George with a pre-Beatle Ringo Starr at The Cavern Club, 1961. As a member of a top local group, Rory Storm and the Hurricanes, Ringo conformed to that band's dapper image.

JOHN LENNON

Street credibility, early-'60s style. Looking lean, mean, and moody in a Liverpool
junkyard, the Beatles promote their first single, "Love Me Do."

Opposite: Ringo is clearly very amused as he attempts another drum-roll,
shortly after being recruited as Pete Best's replacement.

Beatles in Hamburg. Why he was brought into the group to replace Pete Best remains open to conjecture. The reason given at the time was that Pete's drumming wasn't good enough, and that his shy disposition didn't fit in with the quirky nature of the rest of the group. Others who were around have suggested that the ousting was due to McCartney and Harrison's jealousy over Pete's popularity with the female fans. Either way, John, Paul, and George hardly emerged with any credibility from this episode, and the fact that they got Brian to do the dirty work only emphasized this point.

"That John Lennon had not even dared to face me bit deeply," admitted Pete in his book. "I was closer to him than I was to any other Beatle; I had known him intimately for around four years, which is a long time in a young life, and I was fond of him and had much respect for him."

Speaking to biographer Hunter Davies in 1968, John himself commented: "We were cowards when we sacked [Pete]. We made Brian do it. But if we'd told Pete to his face, that would have been much nastier than getting Brian to do it. It would probably have ended in a fight if we'd told him. . . ."

JOHN LENNON

The Beatles give their all at The Cavern soon after Ringo's appointment, and in
the face of fiery opposition from many of the group's fans, some of whom
would periodically shout, "We want Pete!"

A faithful reproduction of The Beatles performing at The Cavern Club in 1962,
as displayed at the Liverpool-based exhibition, The Beatles Story.

JOHN LENNON

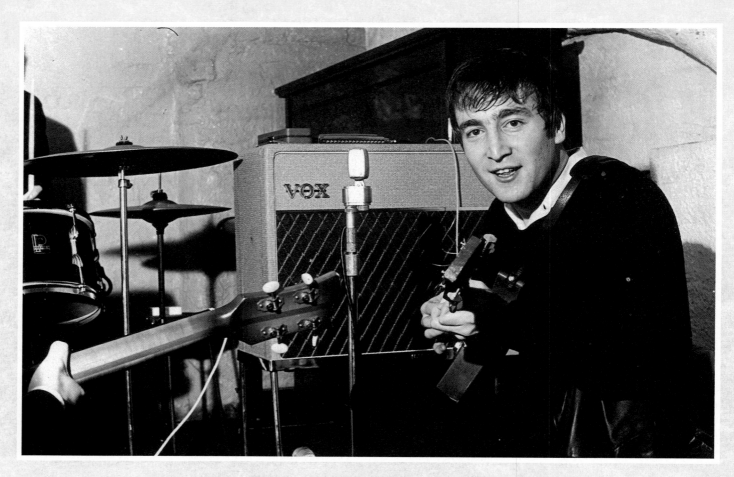

John happily poses for the camera during a late-1962 photo session at
The Cavern. Under Brian Epstein's influence the Beatles became model
professionals, but beforehand they had gained a reputation
for being unruly and unreliable.

This was the contradictory side of John Lennon, a man who could face up to a situation one minute and run for cover the next. In his defense, it must be made clear that this was a trying time for him. In her book, *A Twist of Lennon,* Cynthia remembers that, not long before, she had told him that she was pregnant, and John, a man with an offbeat outlook but old-fashioned values, had immediately responded, "There's only one thing for it, Cyn, we'll have to get married."

Facing up to his responsibilities was one thing, but facing up to Aunt Mimi was quite another. Tempted toward cowardice once again, John realized that trying to avoid the unavoidable was useless. He therefore informed her of the situation and then had to shield himself from the moans and screams about "this disgusting carry-on," as well as put up with her refusal to attend the wedding.

Mimi didn't realize what she would be missing. When the big day arrived, August 23, 1962, the scene that greeted Cynthia inside the registry office more closely resembled a funeral. John, Paul, and George, wearing black suits, white shirts, and black ties, all looked pale and nervous, the registrar appeared as happy as an undertaker, and Cynthia's brother and sister-in-law seemed unsure about the whole situation.

What was needed here was something to liven up the atmosphere, and it wasn't long in arriving. As soon as the marriage service began, a workman outside took this as his cue to go mad with his pneumatic drill! Not a word could be

JOHN LENNON

No. 64 Mount Pleasant, the former registry office where, on December 3, 1938,
Julia Stanley married Freddie Lennon and, on August 23, 1962,
their son John wed Cynthia Powell.

JOHN LENNON

Fans queue almost the length of Mathew Street in September of 1962, prior to a
lunchtime session at The Cavern. Such sights were commonplace during
1961-63, when the Merseybeat boom was at its height, but after the Beatles
and many of their peers departed the scene, things were never quite the same.

JOHN LENNON

The soon-to-be Fab Four rehearses at The Cavern in September 1962. At this
stage Ringo was still using Premier drums with his own name pasted on the
bass skin, but shortly hereafter he would use a Ludwig kit
bearing an early Beatles logo.

heard inside the office, and so as soon as the vows had been taken and the forms signed, the small party, led by Brian Epstein, braved the rain outside and rushed around the corner for the wedding "reception."

This, in actual fact, took place in the less than magnificent setting of Reece's Cafe, a crowded snack bar that offered the newlyweds and their guests a memorable menu of soup, roast chicken, and trifle (fruit and custard spongecake), washed down with glasses of delicious water. Brian paid for the meal, and as a wedding gift he offered the couple his nicely furnished apartment, which was situated near to the Art College.

One thing was for sure: Nobody who was present that day would ever forget it. Least of all John, for as Cynthia accurately observed in *A Twist of Lennon,* referring to the noise of the pneumatic drill, John "had not only gained a headache, he had gained a wife and the promise of a child in only eight months – possibly a bigger headache."

As it turned out, there would be plenty of other things to occupy John's mind in the meantime, not the least of which was the career problem of being a married teenage idol. John was worried that this conflict of image might ground his career just as it was about to take off, and so for the next couple of years Cynthia and child would remain firmly in the background.

JOHN LENNON

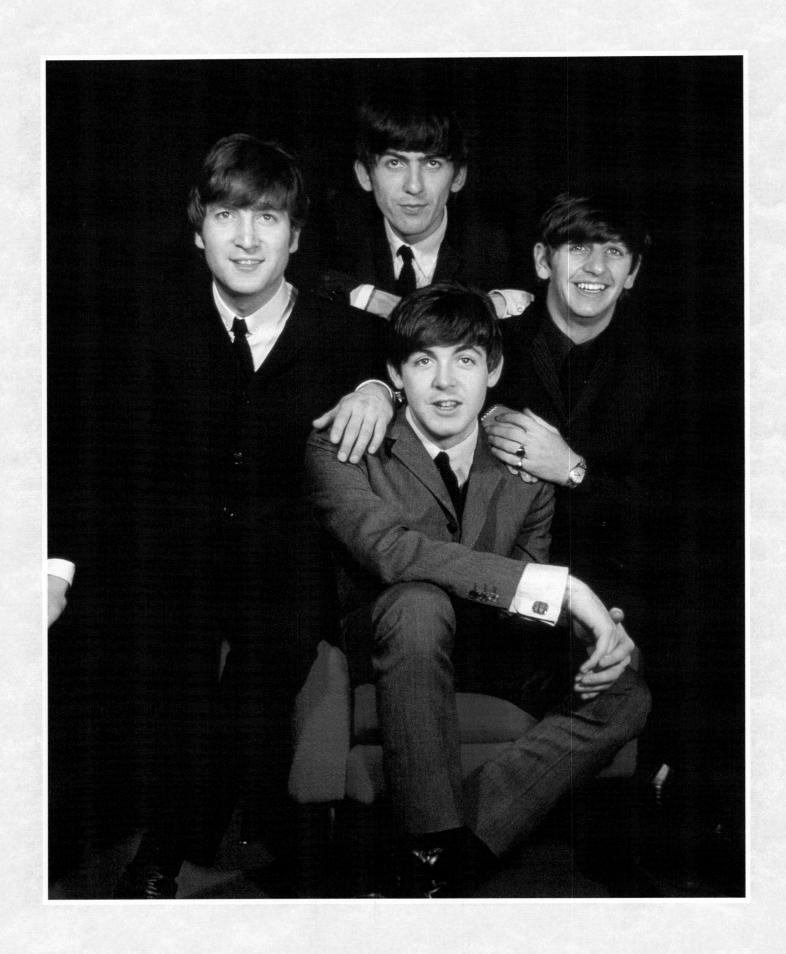

CHAPTER 6

SUCCESS IN HIS OWN WRITE

"For our last number I'd like to ask your help: Would the people in the cheaper seats clap your hands . . . and the rest of you, if you'll just rattle your jewelry."

JOHN LENNON AT THE ROYAL COMMAND PERFORMANCE
November 4, 1963

Opposite: The advance guard of the "British Invasion" that would shake up the American rock music scene in early 1964. With the Kennedy assassination barely two months in the past, Americans were glad to have their spirits lifted by the Beatles' high energy and cheeky good humor.

Above: George Martin, the man who
signed the Beatles to EMI's Parlophone
label, and who produced most of their
recordings during the next seven years.
Opposite: A typically wooden 1963
publicity shot, illustrating the fact that John
did indeed wear glasses. One wonders if
John's old friends in Liverpool were
convinced by this Brian Epstein-cultivated,
happy-go-lucky image.

The John Lennon who rose to fame in Britain as the "leader" of
the Beatles in 1963 was very different from the character
familiar to those who knew him in and around Liverpool.
Instead of the rough-looking, tough-talking, rocker-cum-drifter,
the British public was presented with a smartly dressed,
pleasant, smiling, happy-go-lucky personality; sharp and
challenging, but not too threatening.

As the image of John and the rest of the Beatles was
"upgraded," so too did the group's career get a tremendous
boost. The initial contract with EMI promised limited financial
rewards for John and the others, but it did lead to what would
become a tremendously fruitful relationship with producer
George Martin.

Poised and self-assured even as a very young man, Martin
had joined EMI in 1950, as assistant to A & R (Artists &
Repertoire) executive Oscar Preuss. Together, they toiled for
Parlophone, an EMI label for which the parent company had
nothing but disdain. Throughout the 1950s, Parlophone
releases – largely recordings by bland orchestras and crooners
– were expected by EMI to sell in absurdly small numbers –
and did. Oscar Preuss retired in 1955 and Martin – at 29 –
became head of the Parlophone label. By the late fifties Martin
and Parlophone had found some success with comedy records
featuring the likes of Peter Sellers and Flanders & Swann, but
musical success remained elusive.

Martin had studied piano and oboe, and had once worked
for the BBC Music Library. Rock 'n' roll was not his sort of
music, but he dutifully signed rock artists to his label beginning
in the late fifties. John and the rest of the Beatles met Martin
for the first time on June 6, 1962. The producer was not
convinced of the band's commercial potential, and had no
doubts at all about what he perceived to be the musical
shortcomings of drummer Pete Best. Martin might have been
content to allow Pete to stay on, and substitute an anonymous
session drummer for recordings but, as seen in the previous
chapter, other forces conspired against Best.

So it was that, with Ringo Starr as the newest Beatle, a

JOHN LENNON

John indulges himself in a little body English during a BBC radio recording
session at London's Playhouse Theatre in the summer of 1963.

JOHN LENNON

The tie is off during rehearsals for a TV appearance on the legendary British
rock show, *Ready Steady Go,* on March 20, 1964.

JOHN LENNON

With EMI's U.S. subsidiary, Capitol, at first reluctant to issue the Beatles' recordings in the U.S., more nondescript labels initially took up the challenge.

The photo used on the sleeve of the Beatles' first album was shot at the London headquarters of EMI Records.

simple Lennon-McCartney composition called "Love Me Do" was released in Britain in October 1962. The record sold well in Liverpool from the start and slowly found an audience throughout the rest of the nation. Modest airplay on the BBC eventually pushed "Love Me Do" to #17 by December.

The severe British winter of 1962-63 was brightened by the January release of the Beatles' second Parlophone single, "Please Please Me," another Lennon-McCartney composition. It reached #2 on the British charts by the middle of February 1963, and by the end of the month the record was #1. The Beatles had arrived. The group's first album, entitled *Please Please Me,* was quickly but shrewdly produced, to capitalize on the success of the title track. Among the LP's 13 other cuts

were "Misery," a remarkable version of "Twist and Shout," "I Saw Her Standing There," and "Do You Want to Know a Secret?"

The album and its accompanying publicity suggested that the Beatles were happy, peppy, and well-behaved. From the beginning, John felt stifled by this image, but he was prepared to compromise himself in order to achieve the success that he and his colleagues had fought for so long and hard. He would give interviews, pose for photos, sign autographs, and shake hands with people for whom he often had little time. The sharper side of his nature was never far from the surface, however, and the public would get small glimpses of this on the occasions when he would accidentally (or, sometimes, intentionally) let his guard down.

JOHN LENNON

Standing in his Liverpool record store, NEMS, Brian Epstein proudly shows off a
copy of the *Please Please Me* album, released in the U.K. on March 22, 1963.

JOHN LENNON

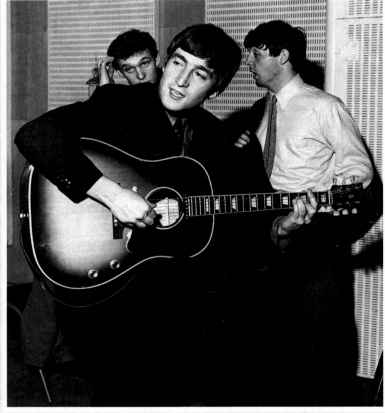

This page, clockwise from left: John, with the Beatles' road manager, Neil Aspinall, and Paul, at EMI's recording studios in Abbey Road, 1963; John and George shop for guitars on the eve of their breakthrough to international success; the "brainy Beatle" shows his athletic nature.

Opposite: Pop stars almost always smiled back in the early '60s, even when they were supposedly relaxing at home!

JOHN LENNON

JOHN LENNON

The prolific and highly successful Lennon-McCartney songwriting team provided the Beatles with a stable power base, and a wealth of proven hit material for other artists to cover.

Cavern deejay Bob Wooler came face to face with John's less-pleasant side when he was beaten up by him at Paul McCartney's 21st-birthday party. A couple of days later Wooler received this apologetic telegram, probably instigated by Brian Epstein.

"The Beatles' first national [British] coverage was me beating up Bob Wooler at Paul's 21st party, because he intimated I was homosexual," John recalled in a 1980 conversation with the BBC's Andy Peebles. "I was very drunk and I hit him . . . and that was in the *Daily Mirror.* It was the back page, I remember the picture."

The story began uneventfully enough. Shortly after Cynthia had given birth to their son, John Charles Julian Lennon, on April 8, 1963, John had taken off with Brian Epstein for a 12-day vacation in Spain. On their return, gossip around Liverpool was rife as to why John had spent time alone with the Beatles' manager. In interviews given just before his death, John himself asserted that his friendship with Epstein had been platonic and that, ever curious, he had simply set about discovering how a homosexual man thought and behaved, at a time when such a subject was still cloaked in mystery.

"We used to sit in a cafe in Torremolinos looking at all the boys," John told *Playboy*'s David Sheff, "and I'd say 'Do you like that one, do you like this one?' I was rather enjoying the experience, thinking like a writer all the time: 'I am experiencing this,' you know."

Talking to the late Roger Scott on London's Capital Radio, Paul McCartney gave his own view of the situation: "John, not being stupid, saw his opportunity to impress upon Mr. Epstein who was the boss of this group. And I think that's why John went on holiday . . . he wanted Brian to know who he should listen to in this group. . . ."

Whatever John's reasons, when the Cavern deejay, Bob Wooler, sidled up to him at Paul's birthday party, held on June 18, 1963, and insinuated that he was gay, he made a double mistake: John was not only insulted, but he was also drunk. The demon liquor always brought out his aggressiveness and, realizing this, he would pretty much stay away from it throughout the Beatle years.

"He never really got into much that was vicious or hard," says his ex-Art College friend, Bill Harry. "He didn't know what it was like to live in a really tough area. I mean, Menlove

(continued on page 93)

JOHN LENNON

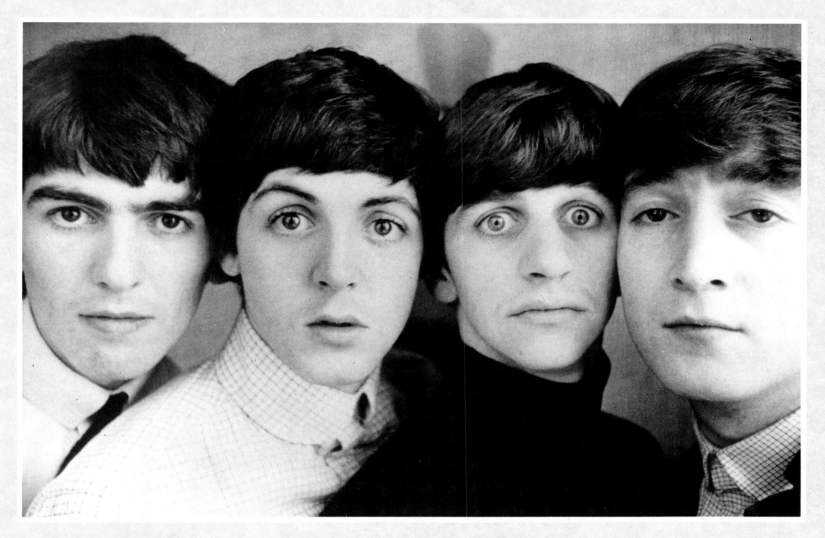

The quiet one, the baby face, the clown, and the cynic, 1963.

JOHN LENNON

Above: Four moptops, sporting the Pierre Cardin collarless jackets that sparked a fashion craze in Britain in 1963. *Below:* Singing "Tell Me Why" during the concert sequence near the end of *A Hard Day's Night.*

JOHN LENNON

Cute but contrived publicity photos were the order of the day during the first flush of Beatlemania. Here, Paul, Ringo, John, and George pause for a bit of refreshment, giving Coca-Cola plenty of priceless free advertising.

JOHN LENNON

Shortly before the Beatles hit America, they appeared on a bill at The Tower in
New Brighton, England, with legendary rocker Little Richard, one of the
American artists whose music had a profound influence on John.

JOHN LENNON

The well-groomed, 22-year-old hitmaker, on the verge of superstardom.
In terms of appearance, at least, John had come a long way
from his days as a leather-clad Teddy boy.

JOHN LENNON

JOHN LENNON

Avenue? He beat up Bob Wooler when he was drunk, but Bob couldn't hurt a fly! You couldn't say that was being tough. Over the years there have been these stories of how fights would break out at some of the venues that the Beatles played in Liverpool in the early days, but more often than not they probably ran as fast as their legs could carry them. So in John's case, I think the toughness was just a cover."

Certainly, for the most part, John was a press agent's dream – the one who, when faced with a microphone, a camera, or an audience, would inevitably come up with a witty remark. It was he who invited the Royals to rattle their jewelry at the Royal Command Performance, who autographed a fan's concert program "Sodoffy from John Leper," and who responded like lightning to the reporters' questions when the Beatles arrived at Kennedy Airport, New York, on February 7, 1964.

Q: "Why does your music excite people so much?"
John: "If we knew, we'd form another group and
    be managers."
Q: "Why do you sing like Americans and talk like
    Englishmen?"
John: "It sells better."
Q: "Was your family in show business?"
John: "No, but I'm told my dad was a great performer."

Retorts like these confirmed to the American public that the Beatles would more than live up to all the publicity hype that had preceded their arrival in the U.S.; the group's subsequent appearance on CBS-TV's *The Ed Sullivan Show* put them over the top in America. Not only did they make great records and have strange haircuts, but they also had interesting personalities, none more so than John.

"Looking back on it with John, you know, he was a really great guy," Paul McCartney told *Rolling Stone* in 1987. "I always idolized him. We always did, the group. . . . He was like our own little Elvis in the group. Not because of his good looks or his singing – although he was a great singer – just his personality. He was just a great guy. Very forceful guy. Very funny guy. Very bright and always someone for us to look up to."

Opposite: By 1964, American talent impresario Ed Sullivan had been catering to—and shaping—America's tastes in TV entertainment for more than 15 years. The Beatles' February 9, 1964 appearance on *The Ed Sullivan Show* was a smashing success, and signaled to an estimated 73,000,000 Americans that John, Paul, George, and Ringo were something special. Here, the Beatles (sans George, who was back at the hotel with a suspected bout of the flu) meet with Sullivan during morning rehearsals on the day of the telecast.

Above: When John's name appeared on the screen, the caption below it stated, "Sorry girls, he's married!"

JOHN LENNON

Beatlemania hits the U.S. as the Fab Four touch down at New York's
Kennedy Airport on February 7, 1964.

Above, left: At an April 23, 1964 birthday party for singer Roy Orbison, John
accepts a forkful of cake from Orbison's wife, Claudette. *Above, right:* A bit of
clowning in Bel-Air, California in August of 1964, during the Beatles'
first full U.S. concert tour.

JOHN LENNON

Fame meant that the Beatles' privacy was a thing of the past. Whether at press conferences (*above, left*) or in the proximity of enthusiastic fans (*above, right*), the group was always the focus of attention.

February 22, 1964: Beatles records played over Heathrow Airport's public address system as British fans turned out to welcome their heroes home from the States.

JOHN LENNON

Early Beatles hits from 1963-64 are leagues ahead of the ragged recordings the group had prepared for their Decca audition just a couple of years before. The single shown above is one of many bootleg issues of the Decca material.

Musically, by the time the Beatles hit America they were in full flow, and the group was riding the crest of a wave on the back of new Lennon-McCartney hits such as "I Want To Hold Your Hand," "She Loves You," "All My Loving," and "From Me To You." These were phenomenal compositions coming from a pair of young unknowns. Equally remarkable was the Beatles' standard of musicianship on these records, thanks in no small part to the polished contribution of producer George Martin. Listening to these tracks, it is almost unthinkable that it is the same group that had performed in such shoddy fashion on the (since widely bootlegged) Decca audition tape just a couple years earlier.

John, for his part, contributed the distinctive harmonica sound that characterized many of the early Beatles recordings,

as well as piano and rhythm guitar. As a guitarist he was never quite in the league of George – or, for that matter, Paul – but he nevertheless turned in some memorable performances: That's John playing the super-fast chords ("triplets") throughout "All My Loving," really helping to drive the song along.

John's main musical asset, however, was of course his tremendous rock voice, full of energy and raw aggression. Paul was by no means an also-ran in this department either, as evidenced by his fantastic renditions of numbers such as Little Richard's "Long Tall Sally," but in John he was up against one of the all-time great rock 'n' roll vocalists.

During the first three years of the group's wide-scale popularity, the Lennon vocal cords would be put to remarkable – and strenuous – use on a string of solid cover versions of

JOHN LENNON

Running through a harmonica part in Studio 2, 1963. The instrument gave
early Beatles recordings a distinctive sound, but John eventually felt its use
was an embarrassing gimmick.

JOHN LENNON

Four young female extras enjoy getting their hands on the Fab Four on the set
of *A Hard Day's Night*. The girl attending to George is his future wife,
Patti Boyd, who can be glimpsed in the movie.

old favorites, including "Twist and Shout," "Money," "Slow Down", "Rock and Roll Music," "Bad Boy," and "Dizzy Miss Lizzy." The manner in which he attacked these songs – moving between a low-pitched growl and a full-tilt scream – was unsurpassable, and he also displayed superb range and versatility. Not that he himself acknowledged this, for as with many other famous singers John was often embarrassed by the sound of his own voice, and he would ask George Martin to tone it down in the mix in order to cover up what he regarded as his inadequacies.

"Listen to 'Twist and Shout,'" he told Jann Wenner in a *Rolling Stone* interview in 1970. "I couldn't sing the damn thing, I was just screaming." Never mind that he had turned in

what is widely regarded as a legendary performance, recorded in just one take! Countless rock vocalists have wished they could "scream" half as well.

As Beatlemania went into overdrive, as British popularity turned into international fame, and as each of the Fab Four became household names, John took everything in his stride. He sailed through The Beatles' first – and best – film, *A Hard Day's Night,* won over the hearts and minds of the people in the street and those in the royal palace, and all the time tried to remain true to himself.

A Hard Day's Night turned the Beatles into bona fide movie stars, and brought an added dimension to their fame. Directed in a breezy, freewheeling style by an expatriate American,

JOHN LENNON

The royal world charity premiere of *A Hard Day's Night* at the London Pavilion cinema, July 6, 1964, was attended by Princess Margaret and Lord Snowdon.

JOHN LENNON

A tanned John and Cynthia, together with George and new girlfriend, Patti,
return to London's Heathrow Airport on May 26, 1964,
after a three-week vacation in Tahiti.

Backstage at the Coventry Theatre, November 17, 1963. Ringo is clearly
ecstatic about applying his makeup.

Above: Moments after this gag photo was snapped in South London on June 3,
1964, Ringo collapsed from the effects of tonsillitis and pharyngitis. Session
drummer Jimmy Nicol took Ringo's place during the first leg of the band's world
tour, scheduled to begin the following day.

Opposite: The debonair John, March 1964.

JOHN LENNON

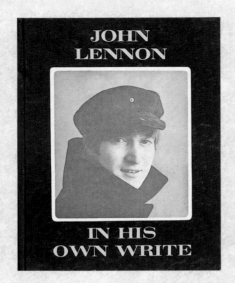

Fans and literary critics were delighted with John's first book, a collection of poems, prose, and drawings published in early 1964.

An Italian-language edition of *In His Own Write.*

Richard Lester, the film chronicled the group's adventures on a supposedly typical day. The movie was a critical success and a box-office smash, and helped to solidify the Beatles' happy, irreverent image. Beatlemania grew even more robust than before.

John was constantly amused and bemused by the power that the Beatles held over their loyal fans, and he would regularly poke fun at this by going into his "Hitler routine": Appearing on hotel balconies, holding a comb over his top lip and giving a Nazi-style salute to the crowds below; and, when about to introduce the next song during a concert, shaking his hands in the air, looking up to the heavens and shouting out a stream of unintelligible words. At other times, he would simply order the thousands of screaming girls to "shut up!"

In early 1964, urged on by Brian Epstein, John delved back into his past to come up with a volume of his poems and drawings, called *In His Own Write.* (This title had been thought up by Paul, whose original idea, *In His Own Write and Draw* – a pun on "right hand drawer" – was considered too complicated.)

Meanwhile, the stack of John's work that Bill Harry had tucked away in his own drawer had been lost when his magazine, *Mersey Beat,* had moved its offices. Therefore, when John contacted him to ask for it back, Bill had to set off around Liverpool in order to track down what he could find.

"I managed to trace Rod Murray, who had shared the flat in Gambier Terrace with John and Stuart," recalls Bill. "He told me that when they had left the place to go to Hamburg, they did so without paying their share of the rent, and so Rod was left to pay this for them. Among John's belongings, however, he had found his exercise book – *The Daily Howl* – and he told me that he would return this when he got the money he was owed in back rent. I relayed this message to Brian Epstein, and he in turn got his solicitor on the case and got *The Daily Howl* back."

Rod Murray had his money, John had much of the material that he needed for his book, and so everyone was happy. But

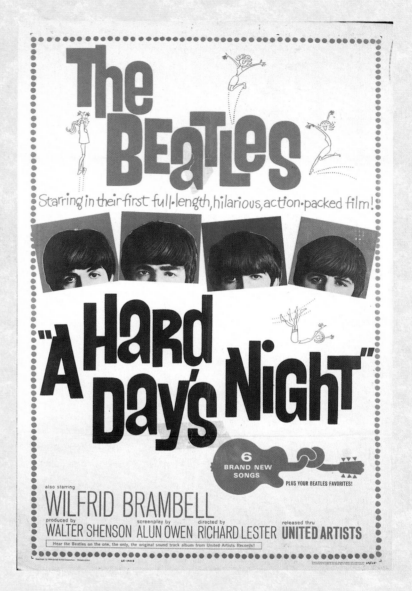

This Pathé News short subject captured backstage scenes and part of the Beatles' November 20, 1963 concert at the ABC Cinema in Ardwick, Manchester, England. In spite of the British accents, isn't "Ya! Ya! Ya!" carrying things a little too far?

"You've heard the song, now see the film!" The *A Hard Day's Night* movie poster, presented with typical mid-'60s graphic style, and focusing on those four "shaggy" hairstyles.

JOHN LENNON

Gloomy faces in Paris, January 1964, possibly reflecting the lukewarm reception
accorded to "Les Beatles" by the French press and public. Press Officer
Brian Sommerville is visible between Paul and George.

Rod had been shrewd. On August 30, 1984, another unique copy of *The Daily Howl* surfaced at an auction at Sotheby's in London, and fetched a staggering £16,000 ($30,000). The vendor? A certain Rod Murray!

In His Own Write, with its nonsense prose, loony poems, daft drawings, and sharp wit, shot straight to the top of the bestseller lists, and drew solid praise from even the most respected of critics: "It is worth the attention of anyone who fears for the impoverishment of the English language and the British imagination," asserted *The Times Literary Supplement.*

Certainly, it chose as its subjects many well-known personalities and issues of the day – television celebrities, politicians, political events – and sent-up them all with great style. Satire was John's specialty, and in his humorous way he had a dig at serious topics such as racism, social injustice, and family conflict.

Therefore, when he attended the Foyle's Literary Luncheon held in his honor at London's Dorchester Hotel in April of 1964, everyone naturally expected John to make a typically hilarious speech, full of jokes and wisecracks. This, after all, was the man who, in his book, referred to Princess Margaret as Priceless Margarine, the Duke of Edinburgh as the Duck of Edincalvert, and President de Gaulle as Prevelant ze Gaute. All they got, however, were a few mumbled words: "Thank you very much, God bless you," (transformed by the press into the more offbeat "Thank you, you have a lucky face"!)

While those present were disappointed by John's reluctance to speak, what they didn't know was that the "brainy Beatle" was suffering from a hangover as the result of some heavy partying the night before, and he didn't even realize that he would have to make a speech. Still, all this did for most people

JOHN LENNON

John and Cynthia attend a literary luncheon held in John's honor on April 23, 1964.

JOHN LENNON

Gum cards, plastic models, and other memorabilia were commonplace
during the Beatlemania period. Unfortunately, because the licensing
of such merchandise was difficult to control, the band members
didn't always receive their fair share.

was confirm that he was excitingly different ("You never know what he's going to do next!"). Aristocrats jostled with the general public outside the Dorchester, trying to get John's autograph.

One lone voice, going against the tide of popular opinion, was that of the British politician Charles Curran, who stood up in Parliament and cited *In His Own Write* as ample evidence of how poor was the standard of education in Liverpool.

Needless to say, nobody took this too seriously, and the following year John would put pen to paper in order to come up with a second volume, called *A Spaniard in the Works,* featuring the likes of Harassed Wilsod (British Prime Minister, Harold Wilson), Sir Alice Doubtless-Whom (ex-PM, Sir Alec Douglas-Home), and assorted cartoons including one portraying a blind man wearing dark glasses, being led by his guide dog, also wearing dark glasses!

JOHN LENNON

L.G. Wood, a former Managing Director of EMI Records, laughed as he recalled how John invariably showed little respect for authority, adopting a familiar attitude with people no matter how high-ranking their position.

"EMI's Chairman, Sir Joseph Lockwood, was a first class man at handling artists, and every now and then he would throw a dinner at the Connaught [Hotel]," Wood remembered, "inviting the Beatles and their wives or girlfriends, George and Judy Martin, and me and my wife. Now I, along with everyone else, would always address him as 'Sir Joseph,' but the Beatles, of course, would just call him 'Joe,' and I remember one occasion when we were all leaving the Connaught, and John came rushing back in and shouted right across the restaurant, 'Joe, get your bloody Rolls-Royce out of the way!' He had absolutely no concern for the fact that he was talking to the Chairman of a massive great company like EMI! He really was a very natural fellow."

Yet while he was enjoying the initial trappings of success, John was feeling less and less inclined to conform to the image that Brian Epstein, together with the press, had created for the Beatles. He felt that his individuality was being stifled, and so he turned increasingly to his art in order to vent his frustrations.

"I was already a stylized songwriter on the first album," he later told *Rolling Stone's* Jann Wenner. "But to express myself I would write *Spaniard in the Works* or *In His Own Write,* the personal stories which were expressive of my personal emotions. I'd have a separate songwriting John Lennon who wrote songs for the sort of meat market, and I didn't consider them – the lyrics or anything – to have any depth at all. They were just a joke. Then I started being me about the songs, not writing them objectively, but subjectively."

It was at this stage, when lyrics describing less than happy emotions began to creep into his songs, that people close to John started to realize that his life was not progressing as satisfyingly as it seemed. Indeed, by the end of 1964 the novelty of superstardom was already beginning to wear off.

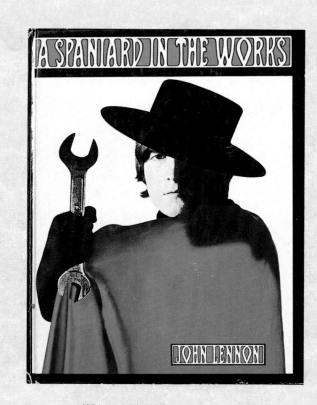

With an initial U.S. print run of 90,000 copies for *In His Own Write*, John was soon being pressured to produce his contracted follow-up. By July of 1965, the result of his efforts was waiting in bookshops for happy buyers.

JOHN LENNON

John and Cynthia take a break from Beatlemania during a 1964 visit to Miami Beach. Soon, though, the grind of touring and dealing with the expectations of fans would take its toll on John and the people closest to him.

CHAPTER 7

NOTHING IS REAL

"Your own space, man, it's so important. That's why we were doomed, because we didn't have any. It is like monkeys in a zoo. They die. You know, everything needs to be left alone."

GEORGE HARRISON
1980
(*I, Me, Mine* by George Harrison)

109

An outtake shot from the Robert Freeman photo session that produced the
beautiful *Beatles For Sale* album cover. The time is late 1964, the place is
London's Hyde Park, and those faces are looking a little tired.

As he became more and more disillusioned with fame, regarding it as superficial and feeling suffocated by it, so John excelled at writing songs that operated on two levels: On the one hand, they were bouncy numbers in the best boy-loses-girl tradition, aimed to satisfy the public's taste; on the other, they contained small insights into his private insecurities.

An early example of this was the self-pitying "I'm a Loser," on the *Beatles For Sale* album, released in Britain at the end of 1964:

> "Although I laugh and I act like a clown
> Beneath this mask I am wearing a frown"

At the time, with Beatlemania at its height, few people – if any – would have noted the true significance of these words,

dropped into the middle of just another catchy number about the heartaches of love. Yet they were written when a constantly packed work schedule was really beginning to catch up with all four members of the group. A non-stop round of television, radio, and film assignments, recording sessions, personal appearances, and concerts around the globe was taking its toll. What had once been fun was now rapidly turning into a sheer money-making exercise.

By 1965, matters were getting worse. John and George, in particular, were growing tired of performing live to hordes of screaming girls who couldn't even hear their music, let alone see them. What's more, with only a few small amplifiers on the stage, the Beatles could hardly hear themselves, with the result that the overall sound was usually atrocious. Adding

JOHN LENNON

John and Cynthia enjoy a day at the beach with the recently married Ringo and
Maureen during a late-spring vacation in 1965. John shows off the well-fed
physique that would later prompt him to look back on this time
as his "fat Elvis" period.

to the boredom, for reasons of their own security they saw hardly anything of the countries that they were visiting; when not working, they were confined to their hotel rooms, so their lives became a dreary succession of airports, hotels, and performance venues. In "Help!," the title song of the Beatles' second movie (directed, like their first, by Richard Lester), John came straight to the point.

> "And now my life has changed
> in oh so many ways
> My independence seems
> to vanish in the haze"

"The whole Beatle thing was just beyond comprehension," he told *Playboy* magazine in 1980. "I was eating and drinking like a pig and I was fat as a pig, dissatisfied with myself, and subconsciously I was crying for help. I think everything comes out in the songs. . . .

"When *Help!* came out, I was actually crying out for help. Most people think it's just a fast rock 'n' roll song. I didn't realize it at the time; I just wrote the song because I was commissioned to write it for the movie. But later, I knew I was really crying out for help. So it was my fat Elvis period. You see the movie: He – I – is very fat, very insecure, and he's completely lost himself. And I am singing about when I was so much younger and all the rest, looking back at how easy it was."

To add to the confusion, John's long-lost father, Freddie, now decided that this was a convenient time to make his grand reappearance. Employed to wash dishes in a hotel

JOHN LENNON

Above: The Beatles' success inspired a wave of "British Invasion" groups. One
of the most successful was London's hard-rocking Dave Clark Five.
Below: Besides handling the Beatles, Brian Epstein (pictured with
George Martin and EMI chairman Sir Joseph Lockwood)
managed other successful British acts, as well.

JOHN LENNON

Above: Diminutive Eric Burdon headed up the Animals, whose earthy sound was born in Newcastle. *Below:* Manchester produced Herman's Hermits, whose perky style bordered on the saccharine.

JOHN LENNON

Above: Lobby cards promoting *Help!*
Titled *Eight Arms to Hold You* during
production, the film's name was later
changed to match the title of
John's composition.

Opposite: John hams it up for a scene from
Help!—or is his appearance a deliberate
hint of things to come? This was the first
time that John sported the famous granny
glasses, even though it would be more
than a year before he would take to
wearing them permanently.

situated only a few miles away from John's Weybridge home, he turned up on his son's doorstep looking like a Bowery bum, clearly in search of a handout. This didn't exactly tie in with John's childhood image of him, as a swashbuckling hero sailing the seven seas.

"Where have you been for the last 20 years?" was the younger Lennon's natural reaction, prompting Freddie to really turn on the hard-luck story: Julia had deserted him, friends and relatives didn't want to know, and somehow, even though he had made good money both as a ship's steward and as a hotel porter, he didn't have two coins to rub together.

John had little time for all this, but right now he was prepared to call an uneasy truce, give Freddie some money, and send him on his way. Yet, the next development in the saga of his "old man" was enough to make John cringe even more: Showing that music was in the blood, "The Ignoble Alf," as his son chose to christen him, released his first (and thankfully only) single, entitled "That's My Life (My Love And My Home)." John, of course, was horribly embarrassed to see all of the coverage that Freddie's record attracted in the music and national press, but at least he had no fears about the competition. Music may have been in the blood, but the talent clearly was not.

On June 12, 1965 it was announced that, purportedly for their services to British industry, the Beatles were to be made Members of the Most Excellent Order of the British Empire (MBE), and on October 26 they received their medals from the Queen in an investiture ceremony at Buckingham Palace. Having originally observed that "I thought you had to drive tanks and win wars to get the MBE," John later confessed that he had seriously considered declining the award, before deciding to go along with it. This way, at least, he would annoy those who had expressed outrage at such an honor being bestowed on "mere pop stars."

"I really think the Queen believes in it all," he said to biographer Hunter Davies, author of *The Beatles.* "She must. I don't believe in John Lennon, Beatle, being any different from

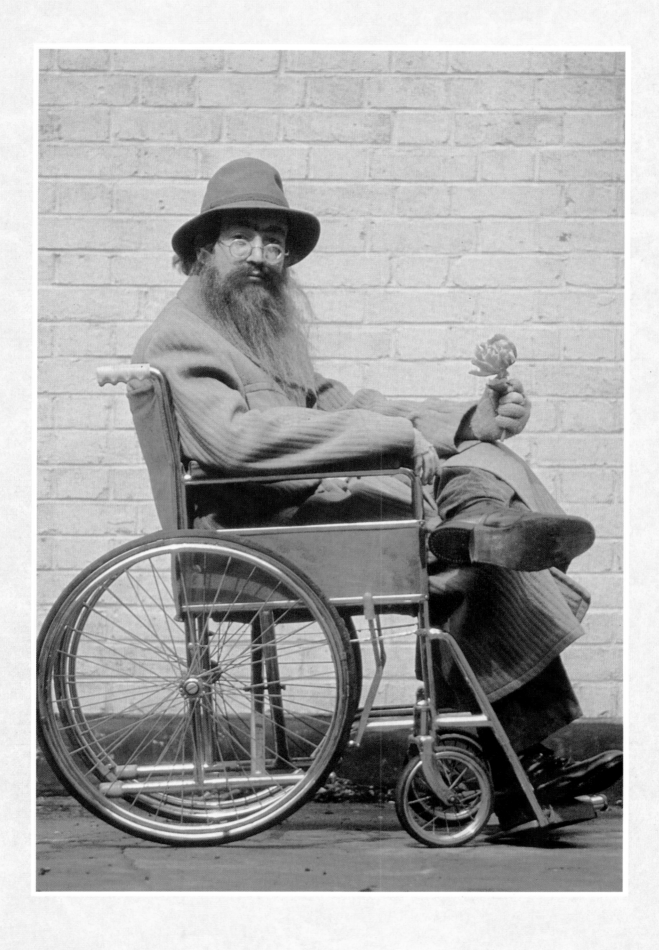

JOHN LENNON

During the last week of January, 1965, John and Cynthia flew to St. Moritz in
Switzerland for a two-week vacation with George Martin and his future wife,
Judy Lockhart-Smith. For John, this was good preparation for
the skiing scenes in the forthcoming Beatles movie, *Help!*

John sports his Bob Dylan cap for the filming of the "Another Girl" sequence
in *Help!* The shoot took place on the island of New Providence
in the Bahamas, during early March, 1965.

A dozen London bobbies arrest four Beatles during a break in the filming of a
scene from *Help!* outside the City Barge pub in Kew on April 24, 1965. Fooling
around with film extras for the publicity camera was still a part of the Beatles'
job, even if the novelty of filmmaking was beginning to wear off.

JOHN LENNON

The Beatles received their MBE medals on October 26, 1965, and subsequently
displayed them inside Brian Epstein's Savile Theatre. After returning the award
just over four years later, John admitted that he had never felt comfortable
about accepting it in the first place.

anyone else, because I know he's not. . . . I always hated all the social things. All the horrible events and presentations we had to go to. All false. You could see right through them all, and all the people there. I despised them."

In the meantime, John played the part of the happily married husband and father. Cynthia and Julian had now come out into the open and family portraits of the three together would frequently appear in newspapers and magazines. In reality, however, John was just drifting, for this was a situation that he found himself in rather than one he would have opted for.

When home, all he really wanted to do was relax and retreat into himself. Alternately watching TV, gazing out of the window,

or reading the books of Swift, Tennyson, Huxley, Orwell, Tolstoy, and Wilde, he rarely got into deep conversations with his wife or played at length with his son. He would, however, feel guilty about his inattention when away on tour, confiding his thoughts in long letters to Cynthia. What he didn't reveal, however, was that his main distractions on the road – as with the other Beatles – were the girls who hung around the band, and an increasing supply of soft and hard drugs.

"'Norwegian Wood' [on the *Rubber Soul* album] was about an affair I was having," he later admitted to *Playboy* interviewer David Sheff. "I was very careful and paranoid because I didn't want my wife, Cyn, to know that there really was something going on outside of the household. . . . I was trying to be sophisticated in writing about an affair, but in such a smoke-screen way that you couldn't tell."

So it is that in the song, after opening with the line: "I once had a girl, or should I say, she once had me," and then telling us:

"I sat on a rug, biding my time,
drinking her wine
We talked until two, and then she said,
'It's time for bed '"

John then cops out by killing the romantic scene and injecting it with some offbeat humor:

"She told me she worked in the morning
and started to laugh
I told her I didn't, and crawled off
to sleep in the bath "

Clearly, then, even though one side of John wanted to keep his privacy, his other, artistic side felt compelled to tell the truth. This would become increasingly apparent over the next few years, highlighting the widening gap between his style of songwriting and that of Paul McCartney.

The *Rubber Soul* album was, in fact, the first clear indication of John's growing maturity as a songwriter, for apart from "Norwegian Wood" he also contributed true classics such as "Girl," the retrospective "In My Life," and the autobiographical "Nowhere Man." These are the sort of mid-period Lennon/ Beatle numbers that, since his death, have been the most frequently played radio-reminders of him. Furthermore, John's recollections of how he wrote them also helps emphasize the often inspirational nature of his talent:

" 'Nowhere Man' . . . I'd spent five hours that morning trying to write a song that was meaningful and good," he told *Playboy* interviewer David Sheff, "and I finally gave up and lay down. Then 'Nowhere Man' came, words and music, the whole damn thing, as I lay down. The same with 'In My Life'! I'd struggled for days and hours trying to write clever lyrics. Then I gave up

"Kenwood," the luxury home the Lennons purchased for £20,000 in July of 1964. John, Cynthia, and Julian lived here throughout the Beatlemania years. It was also here, in 1968, that John and Yoko recorded "Two Virgins" while Cynthia was away.

Overleaf: Beatlemania rocks out. Behind those happy faces, though, was a growing discontent.

JOHN LENNON

JOHN LENNON

An Italian fan makes a grab for John's cap during one of the Beatles' June 1965
performances at the Teatro Adriano in Rome.

and 'In My Life' came to me. So letting it go is what the whole game is."

More and more, John was becoming a home- and studio-bound musician; the idea of touring was turning into a major headache. By 1966, the Beatles' live performances were, for the most part, pretty tired and lackluster, but there was good reason for this. While their growth as concert artists had been stilted by the screams, the oversized venues, and a strict 30-minute format, their recordings were getting ever more sophisticated and complicated.

The situation was, therefore, totally ridiculous: The band that was putting together works of art the caliber of "Eleanor Rigby," "I'm Only Sleeping," and "Tomorrow Never Knows" for the *Revolver* album was at the same time still giving the public unending live performances of less progressive songs such as "Yesterday" and "I Wanna Be Your Man." The band's studio work was difficult to reproduce on stage during those days of relatively primitive concert equipment, and besides, many of the teenage fans had come to shriek, not to listen.

If the Beatles, then, were undecided as to whether or not they should tour again after 1966, two unsavory episodes helped make their minds up for them: First, while visiting the Philippines, Imelda Marcos, wife of the country's dictator-leader, claimed that the band had snubbed her invitation to the royal palace. The fact that they weren't even aware of the invitation didn't seem to matter. The Philippine media turned on the group, death threats were made, security forces were withdrawn, and when the Beatles and their entourage arrived

(continued on page 128)

JOHN LENNON

122

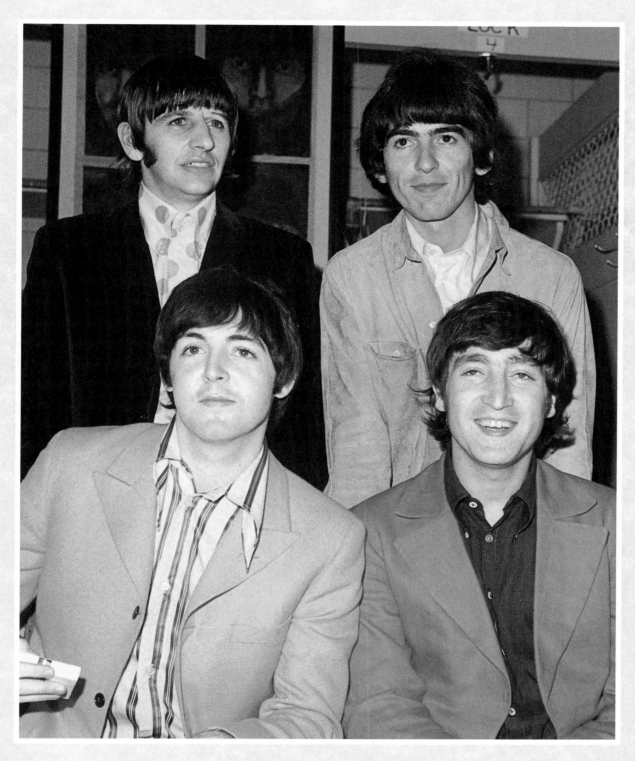

All smiles during a 1966 press conference, but the Beatles' visits to the Far East
and the U.S. during that year were anything but happy. John, in particular,
was learning that fame brought not just acclaim, but harsh criticism.

JOHN LENNON

America embraced the Beatles throughout 1964-65, but John and the others
quickly became fed up with the rigors of touring: unending airports,
anonymous hotel rooms, and the ceaseless din of fans in venues
acoustically ill-suited to music.

JOHN LENNON

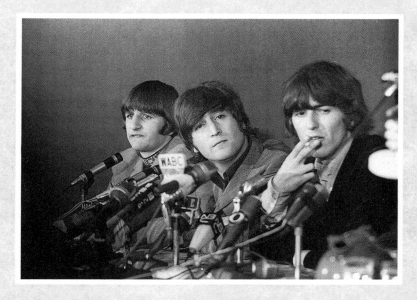

Bored with the same old questions? The Beatles do their duty by meeting the press in New York City on August 15, 1965.

A happy moment from 1964, but after the Beatles stopped touring two years later, Brian Epstein's managerial role diminished, and his personal insecurities increased.

August 11, 1966: Loyal "Beatle People" keep the faith at London's Heathrow Airport as the band departs for its last-ever tour of the U.S. and Canada.

On stage at the Circus-Krone-Bau in Munich, West Germany, June 24, 1966. By this time John was describing the band's concerts as "bloody tribal rites."

JOHN LENNON

Cosmo called him the Beatle with a future . . .

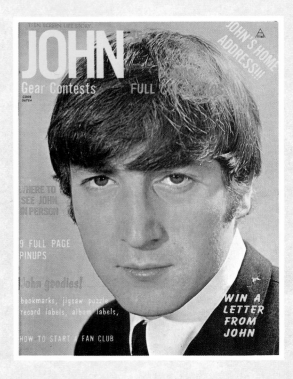

. . . but his fans knew him as simply "John."

Smiling on the outside, tired on the inside.

Looking pensive on the set of *Help!,* April 1965.

JOHN LENNON

Running through "I'm a Loser" prior to taping an appearance on the British
television show *Thank Your Lucky Stars* on November 14, 1964.

JOHN LENNON

The band tapes another appearance on TV's *Thank Your Lucky Stars,*
on March 8, 1965.

at Manila International Airport in order to leave the country, they were kicked, punched, and jostled to the ground. Once they had made it to the aircraft, "immigration problems" delayed take-off, but in the end everything was sorted out and the distressed party continued on its journey.

As if all this wasn't enough, worse death threats were to follow, both for the Beatles in general and John in particular. This time around, John had managed to single himself out by way of an "in-depth" interview that he gave to journalist friend Maureen Cleave, published in the London *Evening Standard* on March 4, 1966. In it, he described his Weybridge lifestyle, his interests in art and reading, and expressed his views on money, politics, and religion.

Influenced by many of the books that he had been reading on the latter subject, John pointed out how the role of the church was dwindling within society, and how people were turning more and more toward material rather than spiritual possessions: "Christianity will go. It will vanish and shrink. I needn't argue about that; I'm right and I will be proved right. We're more popular than Jesus now; I don't know which will go first – rock 'n' roll or Christianity. Jesus was all right but his disciples were thick and ordinary. It's them twisting it that ruins it for me."

Within its true context this was hardly sacrilegious. If anything, John was condemning a situation whereby more people were going to Beatles concerts than attending church.

JOHN LENNON

John adopts the air of a man of mystery during the making of the promotional
films for "Paperback Writer" and "Rain," at Chiswick House in West London,
on May 20, 1966.

As such, the article appeared and was fairly quickly forgotten . . . or so it seemed. On July 29, the American teen magazine, *Datebook,* reproduced the piece with one notable difference: The banner headline incorrectly paraphrased John as saying that the Beatles were greater than Jesus.

This was all that was needed for conservative Americans to raise their voices to denounce the devil-worshiping Beatle. Birmingham, Alabama's WAQY radio led the way as 22 stations banned the broadcasting of Beatles music on their airwaves (never mind that many of the participating stations never even played it in the first place!), and organized several public "Beatles bonfires" at which records, books, and other merchandise relating to the group were tossed into the flames

by people smiling into the assembled press and TV cameras.

Assassination threats were made by some of John's more fervent critics, as were boasts by the Ku Klux Klan that they would disrupt the Beatles' forthcoming U.S. tour. On August 6, 1966 Brian Epstein flew to New York to host a press conference aimed at diffusing the controversy and clarifying John's remarks. But this wasn't enough, and so on August 11, over five months since the interview had been originally published, John and the other Beatles faced the cameras and microphones at the Astor Towers Hotel in Chicago, prior to their two concerts in that city the following day.

In his hotel room before the press conference, John had actually wilted under the immense pressure and, in a rare

Above: A 1966 shot of John, just before he
discarded the moptop image and adopted
the granny specs that would become
his trademark.

Opposite: With his favorite Rickenbacker
guitar.

show of weakness, openly broken down and cried. Now, however, he pulled himself together, and tried to explain his position:

"You know, I'm not saying that we're better or greater, or comparing us with Jesus Christ as a person or God as a thing or whatever it is. I just said what I said and it was wrong, or was taken wrong, and now it's all this. . . .

"When I was talking about it, it was very close and intimate with this person that I knew who happened to be a reporter, and I was using expressions on things that I'd just read and derived about Christianity, only I was saying it in the simplest form that I know, which is the natural way I talk."

This seemed clear enough. Still, one journalist reasoned, he hadn't yet said the magic word: "Sorry." John, although understandably reluctant to do so, was eventually worn down. In the end, he gave in and made the apology that the newsmen were waiting for. Now they were happy, and the whole ridiculous affair could be put to one side.

Not surprisingly, by the end of the tour all four Beatles had decided that enough was enough. No more concerts, no more mayhem, no more aggravation. They were worn out by the grind. More significantly, they were tired of being squeaky-clean. During the past couple of years they had been experimenting with the hallucinogenic drug LSD as a form of escape from all the madness. Fashionable at the time, the drug not only let them "see" things that they had never thought possible, but it also instilled them with a false sense of confidence. John, who was always on the lookout for something new, for some excitement to break up the boredom, took to it like a duck to water.

While, in the long term, the intake of these chemicals may have been destructive, it is undeniable that their effect on John was to lead him in a brand new musical direction and broaden his scope as a composer.

After taking pep pills to keep going in Hamburg, and smoking pot in order to relax during the filming of *Help!,* he discovered that LSD suddenly gave him a whole new outlook on "the

JOHN LENNON

December 1964: John is flanked by actors Dudley Moore and Norman
Rossington, during the filming of a surreal comedy sequence
illustrating his poem "Deaf, Ted, Danoota, (and me)," for the
BBC-TV program *Not Only . . . But Also.*

meaning of life." Combined with the ideas planted in his head by the philosophy books that he had been reading – most notably, Timothy Leary's version of *The Tibetan Book of the Dead* – this helped John produce a true rock masterpiece, "Tomorrow Never Knows."

The song is the closing track on the *Revolver* album. Its heavy psychedelic imagery, strange but interesting sounds – including a guitar solo recorded backwards – and eerie vocals were not only in sharp contrast to the other songs on the LP, but also unlike anything ever heard before.

In an interview that this writer conducted with the Beatles' producer, George Martin, in 1987, Martin recalled: "John wanted me to make him sound like a 'Dalai Lama singing from the highest mountain top,' while still being able to hear what he was singing. Of course, it was an impossible task, except

that he obviously wanted a kooky effect. . . . So what I did was to put his voice through the rotating speaker of a Hammond organ. That gave it the effect you can hear, and to my knowledge that was the first time anyone did that."

Indeed, John did sound as if he were singing into a telephone perched on the top of some far-away mountain, as he invited people to:

"Listen to the color of your dreams
It is not living, it is not living
Or play the game existence to the end
Of the beginning, of the beginning "

So impressed was John with the result of this unorthodox recording technique that soon he came up with an even crazier re-working of the invention: He suggested that he could be

John accepts George's congratulations after passing his driving test on
February 15, 1965. He was never really at ease behind the wheel, though,
and usually preferred to be chauffeured in his Rolls-Royce,
where he could relax in the back and watch TV.

JOHN LENNON

Memorable album sleeves. The semaphore on the *Help!* cover (above, left)
does not spell out the title, but "R," "U," "J,' and "Erase all that has gone before!"
Rubber Soul (middle) signaled the growing maturity of Lennon and McCartney
as individual songwriters, and of the group as musicians. The *Revolver* sleeve
(right) was designed by Klaus Voorman, an old friend from Hamburg,
and future bass guitarist with the Plastic Ono Band.

suspended upside-down from a rope in the center of the studio ceiling, a microphone could be placed in the middle of the floor, and then after being given a quick push he could sing as he went around and around! Needless to say, although George Martin considered this notion to be "interesting," it wasn't actually ever put into practice.

On the same album, the song "She Said She Said" was related to a specific experience of John's, while taking LSD at a Hollywood party. Sitting in a garden, he was approached by the actor Peter Fonda, who reliably informed him that as a result of the pills that he himself had been taking, he actually knew "what it is like to be dead." This was the last thing that

John needed to hear, especially with members of the press hovering nearby, but later on he remembered the episode, played around with it, and translated it into song form:

"She said, 'I know what it's like to be dead,
I know what it is to be sad,' And she's making
me feel like I've never been born"

These lyrics, together with the song's complicated musical structures, were a million miles away from the likes of "She Loves You," recorded less than three years before, and the straightforward rock 'n' roll songs of the 1950s that had inspired the Beatles in the first place. While other artists of

JOHN LENNON

Even though his role in *How I Won the War* is only a supporting one,
John's name was a sufficient box-office draw to earn him co-star billing.

JOHN LENNON

JOHN LENNON

Lunchtime on the set of *How I Won the War* in Carboneras, Spain, in September 1966. This solo project whetted John's appetite for permanent independence from the other Beatles.

Opposite: Private Gripweed in full battle gear on the set of *How I Won the War,* Celle, West Germany, September 1966.

the mid-'60s were also delving into new areas, it was John, Paul, George, and Ringo who led the way. Their progress was truly astonishing, advancing in leaps and bounds from album to album. But John, as restless as ever, was still not really content.

After the band had ended its final tour, he took up movie director Richard Lester's offer to appear in his picture, *How I Won the War,* being shot in West Germany and Spain. This was the first time that one of the Beatles had immersed himself in a full-scale solo project, and later on John was to confess that this experience opened his eyes to a life outside of the group.

"I was always waiting for a reason to get out of the Beatles from the day I filmed *How I Won the War,*" he told *Newsweek's* Barbara Graustark in 1980. "I just didn't have the guts to do it. The seed was planted when the Beatles stopped touring and I couldn't deal with not being onstage. But I was too frightened to step out of the palace."

Still, subconsciously at least, John was thinking of moving on. November 9, 1966, two days after he had returned to England, marked his visit to an exhibit of works by an avant-garde Japanese artist named Yoko Ono. Little did he know at the time, but within a couple of years Yoko would prove to be the stimulus that he was looking for.

JOHN LENNON

CHAPTER 8

MYSTERY TOUR

"I knew that we were in trouble then. I didn't really have any misconceptions about our ability to do anything other than play music, and I was scared."

JOHN LENNON
REFLECTING ON THE DEATH OF BRIAN EPSTEIN
1970
(*Rolling Stone* interview by Jann Wenner)

Opposite: Enormous success encouraged the Beatles to experiment creatively. John, in particular, was eager to explore musical avenues that had been undreamt-of by the Beatles' fans. Here, in a June 1967 candid, he is reassuringly clean-cut and apparently happy . . . but strange things were going on inside that creative mind.

March 30, 1967: Adjustments are made to the setup for the *Sgt. Pepper's Lonely Hearts Club Band* cover shot in the Flood Street, London studios of photographer Michael Cooper. Next to John is designer Peter Blake, behind whose head is a cut-out of Adolf Hitler—a Lennon idea that never made it onto the finished sleeve.

Losing just a little of his enthusiasm for the Beatles, John nevertheless wasn't yet sure of who or what else he could focus his attention on, and so at the end of 1966 he threw himself wholeheartedly into the group's next project, the recording of the landmark *Sgt. Pepper's Lonely Hearts Club Band* album.

This was to set revolutionary new standards in terms of the long-playing record, until that time usually a random collection of commercial songs, some more memorable than others, utilized by the record companies as a straightforward means of gaining more exposure and income for both the artists and themselves. *Sgt. Pepper,* on the other hand, was built around the novel concept of the Lonely Hearts Club Band (guess who) performing a show in front of a live audience. Although many of the album's songs were not originally composed with

this idea in mind, the LP was cleverly packaged so that each cut appeared to fit the format. Overdubbed audience noise added to the overall effect, and these were supplemented by various other sound effects which helped give the record a uniquely fresh and unified atmosphere.

The songs themselves concentrated on a wide variety of subjects that would interest people of the Beatles' age group – sex, drugs, religion, the generation gap – and among John's contributions were some of his strongest compositions to date: One of them, "Being For The Benefit Of Mr. Kite!," featured song lyrics adapted in surreal fashion from a Victorian fairground poster that John had purchased some time before, backed with strange, swirling carousel organ sounds.

"Lucy in the Sky with Diamonds," on the other hand, was a psychedelic musical pastiche that described "tangerine trees,"

An outtake from the *Sgt. Pepper* cover photo session. Contrary to popular myth,
the leaves spelling out the name "Beatles" do *not* come from marijuana plants.

JOHN LENNON

In the control room of EMI's Studio 2 at Abbey Road in early 1967, John listens
to a playback of one of the *Sgt. Pepper* tracks, together with George Martin and,
at far right, technical engineer Ken Townsend.

"marmalade skies," "cellophane flowers," "looking glass ties," "newspaper taxis," and "a girl with kaleidoscope eyes." Yet, contrary to popular myth, John always insisted it was pure coincidence that the initials in the song title spelled "LSD." Instead, the idea for the composition had come from a drawing his son Julian had brought home from school one day, portraying a girl in his class. "What is it?" inquired John. "It's Lucy in the sky with diamonds," came the not-yet four-year-old's reply, providing the perfect offbeat inspiration for his father.

The album's clincher, however, was its final track, "A Day In The Life," penned mostly by John, together with a short passage in the middle by Paul. This rock masterpiece, viewed by some critics as nothing less than a vision of the "Day of Judgment," featured overt drug and sexual references, tidbits of stories that John had heard or read about in newspaper articles, and a 40-piece orchestra providing a finale that had to be, as John put it, "a sound building up from nothing to the end of the

world." The overall effect was (and remains) breathtaking and confirmed that its composer's remarkable musical vision put him in a popular-music class all of his own.

In addition to everything contained on the vinyl disc, *Pepper* also boasted a trend-setting album sleeve, with song lyrics printed on the back (a first), and a front-cover photograph of the Beatles standing in front of a collage of many people whom they considered to be either noteworthy or notorious. These ranged from Hollywood figures Marilyn Monroe, Mae West, and Marlon Brando, to such disparate personalities as Stu Sutcliffe, Bob Dylan, and Oliver Hardy. Inevitably, John had a few other ideas – prize choices that, in the name of good taste, had to be refused or removed from the final setup: Mahatma Gandhi, Jesus Christ, and Adolf Hitler!

In this writer's 1987 interview with L. G. Wood, the former Director of EMI Records (UK) recalled visiting Paul McCartney's house in St. John's Wood, North London (around the corner from Abbey Road Studios), in order to discuss some of the album-cover problems with both him and John. Clearly, the scene that greeted Wood was intended as a good-natured put-on by the two irreverent stars.

"I went into the living room, and there they both were; John was sitting on the end of a couch with a floppy hat on, and doing a bit of knitting – what he was knitting I don't know – and they sat me in a chair, with a colored spotlight shining straight in my eyes! Their attitude was 'Oh, come on then Len, what appears to be the trouble?,' and so I explained to them the problem with using Gandhi and so forth, but of course I ended up leaving them that afternoon really having got nowhere at all!"

Matters were eventually agreed upon, however, and when the album found its way into the record shops in June of 1967, both the disc and its sleeve heralded the start of a new era. The Beatles, for their part, marked the era by sporting their newly sprouted moustaches, and John departed altogether from the Fab Four look by finally getting rid of his contact lenses and donning circular-framed granny glasses. Hereafter, these would become a famous part of the Lennon image, having previously been worn by him in a short sequence of the *Help!* movie, and throughout the filming of *How I Won the War.*

John was now in the midst of a period of unbelievable creativity, not only in terms of quantity, but more importantly with regard to quality. The first track recorded for the *Sgt. Pepper* album, but instead released as a single, was the magnificent "Strawberry Fields Forever," in which John drew on his childhood memories and recounted them as if through a drug-induced haze.

Strawberry Field was, in fact, a Salvation Army home in Liverpool, situated around the corner from the Menlove Avenue house in which John had been raised. He and his school friends would visit the public functions held there each summer; using these experiences as a starting point, John used the song to relate his feelings of loneliness as a youth.

George Martin keeps his eyes on the camera, while "the boys" listen to Paul's run-through of a bass part in EMI's Studio 2 during the *Sgt. Pepper* sessions.

The entrance to Strawberry Field, the Salvation Army home whose summer fetes were attended by John and his friends in the late '40s and early '50s. The building is no longer there, but the gateway and sign have been retained for the benefit of fans and tourists.

John and Cynthia in 1967, drifting in different directions within an increasingly unrewarding relationship. John had already met Yoko, but not yet realized that she held the key to his destiny.

As he explained to David Sheff in a 1980 interview with *Playboy,* "The line says, 'No one I think is in my tree, I mean it must be high or low.' What I'm saying, in my insecure way, is 'Nobody seems to understand where I'm coming from. I seem to see things in a different way from most people.'... At 13, 14, I would think, 'Yes ... I am seeing [somebody's] subconscious; I can read his mind; I'm picking up things he doesn't even know exist. ...' It isn't egomania. It's a fact. ... It doesn't make me better or worse than anybody else; I just see and hear differently from other people, the same way musicians hear music differently from non-musicians. And there is no way of explaining it. ..."

Almost as difficult to explain was the way in which two versions of "Strawberry Fields Forever" – in different keys and different tempos – were spliced together and matched perfectly. John had the idea of joining the first half of the slow version to the second half of the faster one; the only problem was, he didn't have a clue how. Yet when producer George Martin and engineer Geoff Emerick experimented with speeding up one tape and slowing down the other, they found, miraculously, that the different keys came together. Once again, John's insistence on attempting the impossible – along with the invaluable technical assistance of Martin and Emerick – had produced incredible results.

After the release of *Sgt. Pepper* John displayed another side to his songwriting talents: the ability, when required, to turn out an instantly memorable anthem. In this case, the need arose out of a television program called *Our World,* being broadcast live on June 25, 1967, to an estimated worldwide audience of 400 million people on five continents. The Beatles were to represent Britain in the show, and their task was to come up with a new song, simple enough for people anywhere on Earth to understand.

Things were left until almost the last minute, at which point John said, "Oh God, is it that close? I suppose we'd better write something," and came up with "All You Need Is Love." This number, relaying the basic message that, no matter life's problems, "It's easy/All you need is love," was not only adopted as the theme of the "flower power" generation of '67, but has also since become symbolic of the entire decade. Not bad for a spot of quick work!

The Beatles were by now wearing beads, bells, and brightly colored clothes; as if to press home the band's ultra-hip point of view, John even went as far as to have his Rolls-Royce painted in colorful psychedelic patterns. On August 24, he and Cynthia, together with George and Patti Harrison, and Paul and girlfriend Jane Asher, attended a lecture on Transcendental Meditation given by the Maharishi Mahesh Yogi, at the Hilton Hotel on Park Lane in London. The following day, all of them, together with Ringo, turned up at London's Euston Station in order to travel to Bangor in North Wales, where the Maharishi was to hold a weekend seminar. But in the mad dash for the train, amid policemen, press men and hordes of onlookers, Cynthia was left behind on the platform. She tearfully regarded this inadvertent abandonment as an ominous sign of things to come.

Over the past couple of years, she and John had steadily been growing apart, due in no small part to the mental growth that her husband was experiencing through his reading, and through his use of LSD. The drug had little effect on her, but it inspired John to move forward in new directions. In her 1978 book, *A Twist of Lennon,* Cynthia, the loyal housewife, recalled her feelings of helplessness on that August day in Euston Station:

"What nobody could possibly understand was that my tears were not because I had missed the stupid train, but they were expressing my heartfelt sadness. I knew that when I missed that train it was synonymous with all my premonitions for the future. I just knew in my heart, as I watched all the people that I loved fading into the hazy distance, that was to be my future."

Cynthia's feelings of impending doom appeared to be coming horribly true a couple of days later, when word filtered through from London that Brian Epstein had died in his bed

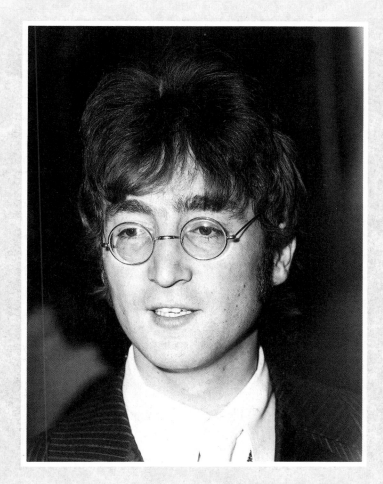

The 26-year-old intellectual and inspirational leader of youth, in June 1967. A halt to the Beatles' incessant touring, together with the band's change of image, brought an end to the hysterical mayhem of Beatlemania.

Sitting next to Maharishi Mahesh Yogi in late 1967, John poses happily for
press photographers. Within a few months, though, he would be
denouncing the giggling advocate of Transcendental Meditation,
both in public and in recordings.

from a barbiturate overdose. He had attempted suicide in 1966 and again in 1967, but because the drugs found in his body after his death were determined to have been ingested over time and not all at once, suicide now seemed unlikely. Whatever the case, the Beatles' tragically troubled manager was gone.

John, initially as shocked as everyone else by the news, knew that this tragedy spelled possible disaster for the Beatles. Regardless, his emotional reaction echoed the response he had years before, when he learned of the deaths of Uncle George and Stuart Sutcliffe.

"[It's] the feeling that anybody has when somebody close to them dies," he explained to *Rolling Stone*'s Jann Wenner in 1970. "There is a sort of little hysterical, sort of 'Hee, hee, I'm glad it's not me'. . . you know? That funny feeling when somebody dies. I don't know whether you've had it, I've had a lot of people die on me. And the other feeling is 'What?'. . . . You know, 'What can I do?'"

The Maharishi offered his own advice on dealing with loss. As John recounted to TV cameras at the time, the Maharishi told the Beatles "not to get overwhelmed by grief, and whatever thoughts we have of Brian, to keep them happy, because any thoughts we have of him will travel to him wherever he is." The irony was that Brian Epstein, the man who believed in the combined magic of John, Paul, George, and Ringo, died at the precise moment when they were learning a philosophy enabling them to survive as individuals.

Paul's answer, meanwhile, was to urge the other three to press ahead with the project that he had been dreaming up, the *Magical Mystery Tour* television movie. The Beatles were to script, direct, and produce the film themselves, but without Brian's guiding hand this was a recipe for disaster. Musically, they hadn't yet put a foot wrong, but when it came to dealing with the world of cinema they were simply out of their range.

"[Paul] came and showed me what his idea was, and this is how it went . . . the production and everything," John recalled for *Rolling Stone* interviewer Jann Wenner. "He said, 'Well,

Sitting in his Savile Theatre in 1967, Brian Epstein, at 32, finds little consolation in being one of the most prosperous show biz impresarios in the world. Fearing that the Beatles were slipping from his grasp, he would die a depressed man a few weeks after this photo was taken. Yet the subsequent, uneven performance of his four proteges—both as businessmen and as collaborators—would perhaps prove that they needed him more than they realized.

JOHN LENNON

On location in Sevenoaks, Kent, England, to shoot the promotional film for "Strawberry Fields Forever," January 30 and 31, 1967. This promo was a forerunner of the videos that are a staple of the music industry today.

here's the segment, you write a little piece for that.' And I thought . . . 'I've never made a film, what's he mean, write a script!' So I ran off and wrote the dream sequence for the fat woman, and all the things with the spaghetti and all that. It was like that."

Basically, what ended up appearing on British TV screens during the 1967 Christmas season was a psychedelic mish-mash. Some of the ideas were horrible failures; others were ahead of their time, similar to the Monty Python brand of humor that was to take off during the next decade. The only aspect of the production that really came up to scratch, of course, was the music, featuring several typically brilliant songs, not the least of which was John's surrealistic master-piece, "I Am The Walrus." With this composition, John's

wonderful talent for bizarre wordplay reached a peak. Drawing inspiration from newspaper stories, everyday occurrences, and favorite books such as Lewis Carroll's *Alice's Adventures in Wonderland,* he conjured up strange, disturbing images full of sophisticated little in-jokes. Indeed, many of the song's lines were pure nonsense:

> "Crabalocker fishwife,
> pornographic priestess,
> boy you been a naughty girl,
> you let your knickers down "

In its entirety, the song's effect remains fascinating. No ordinary mind could have devised it or assembled it in such startling fashion.

JOHN LENNON

June 24, 1967: John, Ringo, and Paul promote the Beatles' June 25th
performance on the *Our World* television program. The show reached an
immense audience, and established the song "All You Need Is Love"
as an anthem of the "Summer of Love."

Yet, a film, undeniably, is made up of many elements, and music is only one of them. When *Magical Mystery Tour* was first screened, it was panned by the public and critics alike. Surprisingly, John appeared to be generally unfazed by this negative reaction, as though his identity as a Beatle was diminishing in importance. Bit by bit he was surrendering his leadership of the group, and allowing Paul to assume the role of chief motivator. John was just marking time, waiting for the next big thing to happen, the next new adventure.

In an interview that this writer conducted with him in 1980, actor Victor Spinetti, who appeared with the Beatles in *A Hard Day's Night, Help!,* and *Magical Mystery Tour,* recalled an incident that took place in December of 1967, which gave a fair indication as to John's state of mind at around this time.

"We were just sitting around, talking and having a drink," Spinetti remembered, "and, referring to the weather, I made a casual remark about how cold it was. John looked at me and said, 'Well, Vic, let's go somewhere that's warmer, then!' Before I knew it, within an hour or so, we were sitting in the back of a car, on our way to the airport, en route to Morocco! Neither of us had a penny on us, but John didn't seem to care. He'd made his mind up, and now he was looking forward to the trip. I've got to admit, however, that when he said 'somewhere that's warmer,' I took him to mean another room, not another country!"

Free-thinking and impulsive, this kind of action was typical of John. Still, it couldn't hold a candle to the momentous decision that he was to make a few months later.

JOHN LENNON

CHAPTER 9

OH, YOKO!

"When I first set eyes on Yoko, I knew that she was the one for John. It was pure instinct; the chemistry was right, the mental aura that surrounded them was almost identical."

CYNTHIA LENNON
1978
(*A Twist of Lennon* by Cynthia Lennon)

Opposite: During the late sixties, John appeared to be the Beatle who had changed most dramatically from the smiling moptop of a few years before. In reality, however, he was simply shedding a phony image and revealing his true persona. He now knew what he wanted, and at the top of his list was Yoko Ono.

6 Mason's Yard, in the center of London,
the former site of the Indica Gallery where
John and Yoko first met on November 9, 1966.

When John visited the Indica Gallery in Central London on November 9, 1966 in order to attend a private preview of an exhibition entitled *Unfinished Paintings and Objects,* it wasn't purely due to artistic interest. More to the point, he had been enticed by the gallery's co-owner, John Dunbar (ex-husband of singer Marianne Faithfull), who had told him about a "happening" that would be taking place there, featuring a Japanese woman from New York in a black bag. As John revealed to *Playboy* interviewer David Sheff, this sounded to him like something to do with sex: "Artsy-fartsy orgies. Great!"

What John saw on his arrival hardly turned him on, however. The Japanese-American woman was certainly there, but instead of being inside a bag she was just walking around, arranging some of the objects that would form part of her display the following day. It was to be an avant-garde exhibition, dealing with progressive, decidedly offbeat art. John soon found himself gazing in astonishment at some of the items: A fresh apple on a stand, priced at £200 (at that time, $480), and a bag of nails, a bargain at just £100 ($240)!

"I thought this is a con; what the hell is this," he later recalled to BBC interviewer Andy Peebles. "Nothing's happening in the bags. I'm expecting an orgy, you know . . . and it's all quiet."

After being introduced to "the millionaire Beatle," the woman handed him a little card that said simply, "Breathe." John, although puzzled, responded politely with a quick pant. Next, his eyes settled on a ladder leading up to a canvas suspended from the ceiling, with a spyglass hanging from it on the end of a chain. Climbing to the top of the ladder, he looked through the spyglass to read a word printed in tiny letters.

"You're on this ladder – you feel like a fool, you could fall any minute – and you look through it and it just says 'YES,'" he told David Sheff in 1980. "Well, all the so-called avant-garde art at the time, and everything that was supposedly interesting, was all negative; this smash-the-piano-with-a-hammer, break-the-sculpture, boring, negative crap. It was all anti-, anti-, anti-.

At home in Weybridge during the summer of 1967, John pursues his lifelong
passion for lazing around and reading. At this point in his private life, John felt
himself drifting, as if waiting for "the next big thing" to happen.

Anti-art, anti-establishment. And just that 'YES' made me stay in a gallery full of apples and nails, instead of just walking out saying, 'I'm not gonna buy any of this crap.'"

The humor in the work, while downright strange to many people, was of a kind that appealed to John's sense of the absurd, and his interest was now taken. Nearby was an object called "Hammer and Nail," consisting of a board with a chain and a hammer hanging on the end, and a bunch of nails positioned underneath. Could he hammer one of the nails in? "No," was the initial reply. Tut, tut! The gallery owner pointed out to the artist that this was no way to treat a Beatle. Besides, with all his money, John might buy the piece!

John told David Sheff in 1980, "So there was this little conference and she finally said, 'Okay, you can hammer a nail in for five shillings [60 cents].' So smart-ass here says, 'Well, I'll give you an imaginary five shillings and hammer an imaginary nail in.' And that's when we really met. That's when we locked eyes, and she got it and I got it, and that was it."

The woman was, of course, Yoko Ono. Seven years older than John and then in the middle of her second marriage, she had turned her back on her middle-class background, and created quite a name for herself with the New York avant-garde set. Now she was attempting to cause a similar stir in London. She would set about her task by, among other things, covering one of the lion statues in Trafalgar Square in huge white sheets, and filming a feature-length movie focusing solely on 365 naked bottoms.

Over the course of 18 months, she and John met on several occasions, and she would also keep in touch by sending cryptic, humorous notes, instructing him to "Breathe" or "Watch all

John's obligatory appearances with the rest of the Beatles continued, as at this
June 1967 press party at Abbey Road studios.

the lights until dawn." At first, Yoko's antics were of passing interest to John, but eventually they had their effect. In time John found that Yoko occupied his thoughts with increasing frequency. Cynthia, meanwhile, was growing steadily more depressed about the fragile state of her marriage.

"Although John said very little about the impression I made as his wife, I always felt that he expected a great deal more of me," she later confessed in her 1978 memoir, *A Twist of Lennon*. "I really wasn't on his wavelength as much as he would have liked. He needed more encouragement and support for his way-out ideas."

On meeting Yoko, Cynthia felt that she had stumbled upon John's solution, even though he himself appeared to be totally ignorant of the possibilities. During an argument, Cynthia even went so far as to suggest that he would be "better off with that Yoko Ono," but John discarded this notion as ridiculous.

When Cynthia went away with friends to Greece in May of 1968, however, John's curiosity got the better of him and he invited Yoko to his Weybridge home. His childhood friend, Pete Shotton, who was by now employed as his personal assistant, was also staying there at the time; he went to bed

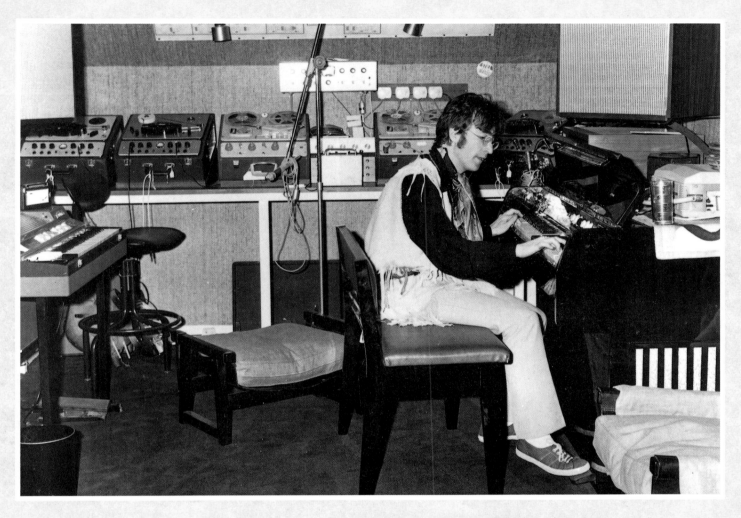

John at work in his home studio at Weybridge in 1967. It was here that he and
Yoko would later collaborate on the *Two Virgins* LP.

early while the two prospective friends retired to John's small home studio, planning to "mess about with tapes" and make some recordings.

The next morning, Pete arose to be greeted by the sight of John sitting in the kitchen in his dressing gown, treating himself to a quick breakfast. Although he confirmed that he had spent a "great night" with Yoko, his mood was strangely quiet and serious, and if Pete sensed that he was building up to something, he didn't have to wait long to discover what it was: John wanted him to find a house that he and Yoko could go and live in!

"It was quite a stunner," recalls Pete. "He came out with this incredible revelation that this was what he'd been waiting for all his life. To hell with everything else, he'd go live in a tent with her if he had to. Here was a guy who was willing to take his entire past up to that moment and just throw it completely out of the window, because he had found what he wanted. I jumped up and said, 'Just like that?' and he said, 'Yeah, just like that. This is what I've been waiting for, Pete!'"

An earlier attempt by John to find peace of mind came in the form of learning the techniques and principles of Transcendental Meditation. Yet, a February 1968 trip to Rishikesh

JOHN LENNON

in India, studying under the Maharishi with the other Beatles, their partners and friends, ended in disillusionment when a rumor spread that the "Mystic One" had tried to force his untranscendental attentions on one of his students, actress Mia Farrow. Once again, John's hopes for a more settled life had been shattered.

"Having gone through all of the Beatlemania, the drugs, the Maharishi and so on, I saw him becoming, if anything, a more incomplete person," says Pete Shotton. "He was getting more and more frustrated with the fact that it wasn't providing him with any great satisfaction in life. And, of course, beyond any shadow of a doubt, the answer to all this was Yoko. She was, quite categorically, the best thing that ever happened to him."

In a piece that ultimately found its way into the 1986 book *Skywriting By Word of Mouth,* John himself described Yoko as "The only woman I'd ever met who was my equal in every way imaginable. My better, actually. Although I'd had numerous interesting 'affairs' in my previous incarnation, I'd never met anyone worth breaking up a happily married state of boredom for. Escape, at last! Someone to leave home for! Somewhere to go. I'd waited an eternity."

When Cynthia returned from her Greek vacation she found herself to be a stranger in her own home. John and Yoko were both there, clearly established as a couple, and there could be no doubt that the time for radical change had arrived. John, having made his decision, appeared totally at ease about the whole situation, and it was Cynthia, in fact, who packed her personal belongings and moved out.

"I didn't blame John and Yoko," Cynthia later asserted in *A Twist of Lennon.* "I understood their love. I knew I couldn't fight the unity of mind and body that they had with each other. . . . Yoko did not take John away from me, because he had never been mine. He had always been his own man and had always done his own thing. . . ."

John's love for Yoko was so powerful, so all-consuming, that it took no account of the pain it might inflict on others; it also took no account of the pain that would be inflicted on them.

Cynthia Lennon's book of sensitively related memoirs found its way into print in 1978, despite John's opposition to its publication.

Opposite: Following a few paces behind George, John strolls the grounds of the Maharishi's camp in Rishikesh, India in February of 1968. While much of John's time here was taken up with songwriting and transcendental meditation, he was also preoccupied with thoughts of Yoko.

LOOK 50 CENTS · JANUARY 9, 1968

A special issue on **Sound and fury in the arts** from sex and violence in the movies to madness in the galleries from Leonard Bernstein to **a pullout portfolio on the Beatles**

CALIFORNIA'S INCREDIBLES from Hippies to Hell's Angels

BEATLE JOHN LENNON BY AVEDON

"Listen to the color of your dreams. . . ." This stunning pop-art photo by Richard Avedon appeared on the cover of an issue of *Look* magazine, and adorned countless bedroom and dorm walls in the late sixties.

Opposite: "I declare these balloons high," says John, as he launches 365 of them into the air above London during the grand opening of his first full art exhibition, *You Are Here,* at the Robert Fraser Gallery in 1968.

John saw Yoko fulfilling the roles of friend, wife, lover, teacher, mother; someone with the same views, the same outlook, the same taste for the bizarre – "Me in drag," as he once put it. The British press and public, on the other hand, had a distinctly different impression of her. What was the leader of the Fab Four doing, deserting his loving, faithful wife and taking up with this strange, mystical, Oriental woman who dabbled in all forms of weird but not-so-wonderful art?

John and Yoko's first public "event" together, on June 15, 1968, was the planting of two acorns in the grounds of Coventry Cathedral, one facing east, the other facing west. The planting was intended as symbolic of their meeting and love for one another, as well as the uniting of their two cultures. John regarded the world of conceptual and avant-garde art as a refreshing change from the commercially driven pressures of Beatlemania, and, following Yoko's lead, he was bubbling over with ideas that matched hers.

Three days later, the two of them turned up at London's Old Vic Theatre to attend the opening night of the National Theatre's stage production of part of John's book, *In His Own Write.* Their presence really set the reporters' tongues wagging in the following morning's national newspapers. Needless to say, the journalists all made sure that they were at the next grand opening that would be attended by the "odd couple," this being John's first full art exhibition, held at The Robert Fraser Gallery on July 1. Entitled *You Are Here,* it contained a Yoko-inspired mixed bag of odd objects; John kicked off the proceedings by cutting a string and allowing 365 helium-filled white balloons to float up into the London sky. Attached to each was a note stating: "You Are Here. Write to John Lennon c/o Robert Fraser Gallery, 69 Duke Street, London W1."

People responded, all right, but hardly in the way that John had been expecting. While the critics looked at the exhibition and shouted "rubbish!" the balloon cards arrived in the hundreds, telling John to go back to his wife and criticizing a whole catalogue of things: Yoko, John's long hair – which he had center-parted in a style resembling Yoko's – his wealth,

JOHN LENNON

JOHN LENNON

The 1968 feature-length cartoon, *Yellow Submarine,* was described by one critic
as "the best film the Beatles never made."

Opposite: Yoko, Julian, and John, 1968.

and his nerve at daring to cross over into the world of art. John was genuinely shocked and disappointed by all of this.

"The trouble, I suppose, is that I've spoiled my image," he confided to a reporter. "People want me to stay in their own bag. They want me to be lovable. But I was never that. Even at school I was just 'Lennon.' Nobody ever thought of me as cuddly!"

Worse, however, was to follow. Everywhere that John and Yoko went, people voiced their disapproval by shouting out "Where's your wife?," "Chink!," and other presumptuous crudities. The press, of course, decided to jump on the bandwagon that it had started rolling, by turning on the couple with unprecedented venom. The attacks were both unwarranted and distasteful, often racist in tone; some openly described the love of John's life as "ugly." Because they were highly visible, John and Yoko had become easy targets. Unfortunately even some of the Beatles' fans went along with the ugly mood.

One girl, quoted by Philip Norman in *Shout! The Beatles in Their Generation,* recalled standing with friends outside the EMI Studios in Abbey Road and handing Yoko a bunch of yellow roses, thorns first. Not realizing that this was intended as an insult, Yoko thanked them repeatedly and John said, "Well, it's about time someone did something decent to her."

The net effect of all this ill-will was to put severe strain on John and Yoko's relationship. What had started out as a misty-eyed love affair was quickly turning into a major ordeal, and adding to the pressure were the arguments that were beginning to crop up between all four Beatles during the recording sessions for their new album. Having recently taken a major step in his life, John was clearly going to have to take a few more in order to hold onto his sanity, as well as the love that he had waited so long for.

On August 22, 1968 Cynthia Lennon sued her husband for divorce on the grounds of his adultery with Yoko Ono. John did not contest the order.

CHAPTER 10

PARTING OF THE WAYS

"An exorcism, in one way, is what it was. A clearing of the decks, I think, also. John had to clear the decks of us to give space to his and Yoko's thing."

PAUL McCARTNEY
1987
(*Rolling Stone* interview by Anthony DeCurtis)

Opposite: John plays his stripped-down Epiphone Casino guitar during the "Get Back" sessions at Twickenham Film Studios in January of 1969. The music turned out well, but John was more eager than ever to go his own way. The Beatles' days as a group were numbered.

John, Yoko, and 5-year-old Julian in December of 1968, during a break in the
filming of the Rolling Stones' unscreened TV special, *Rock and Roll Circus*.
Stones member Brian Jones is at far left; Eric Clapton sits next to John.

Heads turned and eyebrows were raised when John dared to bring Yoko with him to the Beatles' recording sessions. Beatle wives and girlfriends normally stayed firmly in the background, taking care of the home or the children, and coming out into the open only when there was a suitable occasion, such as a showbiz party. The studio was where the men worked and played; this was the way it had always been and, no doubt, the way it was going to stay.

Yoko, on the other hand, was in no way prepared to settle for the unrewarding role of "the little woman." An extremely forceful character, she had forged her own career in the world of avant-garde art, and if John wanted to be with her then he would have to accept her on equal terms. Never mind his star status; she'd hardly even heard of him before they first met! For a man who, all his life, had been accustomed to women always being there to serve his every whim, Yoko's attitude was a real eye opener.

"Yoko was a very liberated woman," says Pete Shotton. "She considered herself, quite rightly, to be as good as anybody else whether they be male or female, and she was damned well not going to be treated like a 'Beatles woman.' That was half the beauty of it all: Someone had stood up to John and said 'No' to him!"

"You have to remember that John, like myself, came from a completely male-dominated environment back in Liverpool," adds Bill Harry. "The girls were generally very meek, and many of them would do whatever the boyfriends said. This continued when they got married – the house was the husband's house, the money was the husband's money – and it was a terrible system which still exists to some extent. The girls were like second-class citizens, and they had to dress sexily, not because of their own tastes but because this was the way that the men wanted them. A prime example of this was Cynthia; getting her to dress like Brigitte Bardot and look like Brigitte Bardot and be transformed into a mini Brigitte Bardot, because that's what [John] fancied and that's what she had to do to get him!"

Now, however, the male chauvinist was faced with a tough feminist who demanded as much say and as much attention as he did. What's more, John was so besotted by Yoko that he didn't want to be apart from her for even a few minutes, let alone several days. He had waited long enough to find his soul mate, and now he was going to share every moment with her.

"Even though John was one of the most popular men in the world for quite a long time, surprisingly enough he had no real close friends outside of the Beatles themselves and their very tight-knit circle," asserts Pete Shotton. "John formed very intense relationships with very few people, and that's all that he needed."

There again, the irony of John and Yoko's intense relationship was that while they were both highly individual people, they each seemed intent on submerging their own personality in order to exist as a couple. As John himself often said, "We are one person."

The upshot of all this was that Paul, George, and Ringo were suddenly confronted with Yoko sitting in on their recording sessions. Worse still, she not only tried to join in on some of the songs, but – horror of horrors – dared to offer her own musical suggestions. Needless to say, this didn't go down at all well, and it soon became abundantly clear to John that if he wanted to work with Yoko, then it wasn't going to be within the structure of the Beatles.

In the meantime, he was writing and recording some of his most potent material to date for the group's next album, a twin-record set entitled simply *The Beatles,* (now popularly referred to as *The White Album,* for its pristine white sleeve), released in November 1968. The LP was issued on the Beatles'

Above: The Apple boutique at 94 Baker Street, London, in 1968, complete with the psychedelic mural that irritated neighboring merchants. *Below:* The same building today.

JOHN LENNON

JOHN LENNON

own Apple label, formed at considerable expense in early 1968 as part of an ambitious business enterprise that included two Apple retail stores, Apple Electronics, Apple Films, Apple Management, and Apple Music, the latter the focus of the group's independent recording and publishing company. With Apple, the Beatles hoped to gain full control of their artistic and business destinies.

The lyrics John wrote for songs on *The White Album* were poetic but to the point, and covered a broad range of topics: opposition to American involvement in Vietnam, in "The Continuing Story Of Bungalow Bill" ("He's the all-American bullet-headed Saxon mother's son"); reluctance to support the student riots of 1968, in "Revolution" ("If you want money for people with minds that hate/All I can tell you is brother you have to wait"); the problems of insomnia, in "I'm So Tired" ("You know I can't sleep/I can't stop my brain/You know it's three weeks/I'm going insane"); feelings of depression, in "Yer Blues" ("Black cloud crossed my mind/Blue mist round my soul/Feel so suicidal/Even hate my rock and roll"); and sexual pleasure, in "Happiness Is A Warm Gun" ("She's well acquainted with the touch of the velvet hand/Like a lizard on a window pane").

Then there were songs addressed to people who John knew or had known: the Maharishi, whose name was jokingly disguised as Sexy Sadie, ("Sexy Sadie, what have you done?/You made a fool of everyone"); Mia Farrow's sister, "Dear Prudence," who was constantly meditating when the Beatles and their friends were in India ("Dear Prudence, won't you come out to play?/Dear Prudence, greet the brand new day"); Paul McCartney, who is paid an inaccurate compliment in Glass Onion ("Well here's another clue for you all/The Walrus was Paul"); and John's mother, remembered in the beautiful but haunting "Julia," ("Julia, seashell eyes, windy smile, calls me/So I sing a song of love, Julia").

This last number, in fact, also contained two other revealing lines: "Ocean child, calls me" was a reference to Yoko, whose name means ocean child in Japanese; and the self-explanatory,

Apparent fun and frivolity in the Apple offices in 1968, but no way to run a multi-million-pound business empire. John takes the "hilarity" in stride.

Opposite: July 28, 1968: The Beatles spend the day posing for a new set of promotional photos, shot in and around London. Personality conflicts and mounting business problems were already taking their toll on the group.

JOHN LENNON

"When I cannot sing my heart, I can only speak my mind."

Yet John reserved some of the greatest lyrics he would ever write for a song that was originally intended – and should have been released – as a single, but instead ended up being donated to a various-artists charity disc, before turning up on the *Let It Be* album. The song was "Across The Universe" and the beauty of the poetry and the power of the imagery and wordplay stand as one of the finest samples of the genius of John Lennon:

> "Images of broken light
> which dance before me
> like a million eyes
> That call me on and on
> across the universe
> Thoughts meander
> like a restless wind
> inside a letter box
> They tumble blindly
> as they make their way
> across the universe "

While John plays lead guitar and Paul sings "Get Back," police officers set about bringing a halt to the impromptu concert being performed on the roof of the Beatles' Apple building in Savile Row, Central London, on January 30, 1969. As crowds gathered in the street below, the group's last-ever live performance brought lunchtime traffic to a standstill.

John, typically, was never pleased with the recording or the way that he sang it, but he was particularly proud of the lyrics. "They were purely inspirational and were given to me as boom!" he told *Playboy* in 1980. "I don't own it, you know; it came through like that. I don't know where it came from. . . . It's not a matter of craftsmanship; it wrote itself. It drove me out of bed. I didn't want to write it, I was just slightly irritable and I went downstairs and I couldn't get to sleep until I put in on paper, and then I went to sleep.

"It's like being possessed; like a psychic or a medium. The thing has to go down. It won't let you sleep, so you have to get up, make it into something, and then you're allowed to sleep."

For all of its tremendous music, however, *The White Album* signaled the beginning of the end for the Beatles. Apple Music was an undisputed success but the other Apple divisions were only eating up the Beatles' money, and not producing any –

were not, in fact, even issuing any products. Apple head-quarters was less a place of business than a rendezvous where staffers could eat and drink at their bosses' expense. The Beatles' accountants threw up their hands. Tensions within the group escalated and the members' squabbles, the personal ones and those caused by the troubled Apple empire, manifested themselves in the reality of the Beatles no longer performing together as a group. Instead, each member was only really interested in recording his own songs, and casting the other three in the subordinate roles of session musicians.

They were all growing tired of the setup: Ringo with the unhappy atmosphere; George with the way that his talents were being stifled by Lennon and McCartney; John with Paul's bossiness and self-interest; and Paul with John's eccentric public behavior and his obsession with Yoko.

The two ex-songwriting partners were also becoming irritated by the widening gap in their musical tastes: John felt that a snap-happy tune like "Ob-La-Di, Ob-La-Da" should never have found its way onto a Beatles album. Paul felt that "Revolution 9" had been similarly misguided.

This last-mentioned track wasn't, in fact, a song at all, but instead just a collage of different sound effects combined with assorted snatches of John speaking. Put together by him and Yoko, with George Harrison and George Martin, it was disjointed and certainly the strangest contribution ever to appear on a Beatles record, but at this time it was very much in line with the new "musical" direction that the couple was exploring.

The pair's collaboration culminated in a short series of avant-garde albums, the first and most famous of these being *Unfinished Music No. 1: Two Virgins,* which they had recorded on the night that John invited Yoko to his house while Cynthia was in Greece. Released on November 29, 1968, the disc mainly consisted of the two of them making assorted squawking, screeching, and twittering noises, to the occasional accompaniment of a tinkling piano and slowed-down tape effects. To John it was a progression on the kind of sound

One group, four distinctly individual characters. Tittenhurst Park, August 1969.

John's commitment to Yoko and the relationship he shared with her were intense. Unfortunately, many of John's fans did not embrace his enthusiasm for his new mate.

tricks that he had experimented with on Beatles tracks such as "Rain," "I'm Only Sleeping," and "Tomorrow Never Knows."

Although undeniably novel, *Two Virgins* would have been quickly forgotten had it not been for the infamous cover photographs: On the front, John and Yoko stood together totally naked, facing a remote-controlled camera; on the back, predictably, was a shot of them taken from behind. This sort of unblushing sleeve art would be outrageous even today, but in 1968 it had old ladies reaching for the smelling salts.

John later explained that he and Yoko could have chosen more complimentary photos for the album cover, but the unglamorous ones that were used were intended as a message.

In an RKO Radio interview on December 8, 1980, John recalled, "We wanted to say, 'We met, we're in love, we want to share it.' And it was kind of a statement, as well, of an awakening for me, too. 'This Beatle thing you've all heard about, this is how I am really.' You know, 'This is me naked, with the woman I love. You want to share it?'"

The problem was that not many people *did* want to share it. John, however, couldn't have been too surprised by this response. From his early childhood he had always enjoyed shocking people, and the album sleeve was just another Lennon send-up. The only difference this time around was that instead of his victim being a specific person, he managed to shock the general public.

In the RKO interview, John cast himself in the role of the outraged public, asking, "'What are they doing? This Japanese witch has made him crazy and he's gone bananas!' But all she

John Winston Lennon in 1968. It was a year of notable transition for him, and of great personal triumph.

did was take the bananas part of me out of the closet more, that had been inhibited by the other part. It was a complete relief to meet somebody else who was as far out as I was. . . ."

In many ways, John and Yoko were having a ball, but it wasn't all fun and games. On October 18, 1968, while staying at Ringo's apartment in Montagu Square, Central London, they were arrested for possession of cannabis and obstruction of the police in their execution of the search warrant. John's divorce from Cynthia became final on November 8, and on the 21st he was by Yoko's side in the hospital when she suffered a miscarriage of the baby that she was expecting. A week later, anxious to minimize the possibility of Yoko being deported (she was not a British citizen), John pleaded guilty to the cannabis charge and was fined £150 ($360).

The year 1969 got off to an equally gloomy start. The January film and recording sessions for the doomed *Let It Be* project – during which the Beatles compensated for a lack of inspiration with lots of petty squabbles – brought home the fact that the band that John had started was now little more than a time-consuming burden to him. To make matters worse, the Beatles' business affairs were in such a mess that they were rapidly going broke, and at John's instigation the legendary entertainment business manager Allen Klein was brought in to try to salvage the situation.

New York-based, Klein specialized in securing back royalties for his clients, and convincing record companies to hand over enormous advance fees. His clients had included the Rolling Stones, Herman's Hermits, the Animals, and the Dave Clark

JOHN LENNON

Father and Mother Christmas, aka John and Yoko, at the Apple Christmas
party, December 23, 1968.

JOHN LENNON

172

Allen Klein with John and Yoko in 1969, after the couple had instigated his appointment as the Beatles' business manager. Five years later, John would take Klein to task via the song, "Steel and Glass."

Five. He was tremendously successful, but had also run afoul of the Securities and Exchange Commission in the mid-sixties, after taking control of bankrupt Cameo-Parkway Records and pushing its stock price through the roof by, it was said, instigating untrue takeover rumors.

Regardless, Klein became the Beatles' business manager in the spring of 1969, and soon set about trimming the fat off the Apple. Paul McCartney distrusted him, and his later refusal to be handled by Klein only served to widen the rift within the group. Although the August sessions for the *Abbey Road* album signaled a welcome return to form, John was by now actively pursuing an increasing number of solo projects. His heart was no longer really in the Beatles, for he could work with Yoko and indulge his new musical ideas without having to justify them.

Paul, always the most enthusiastic member of the group, tried hard throughout much of 1969 to rekindle the interest of his three reluctant colleagues, but all he really seemed to achieve as a result of his persuasive efforts was to annoy them even more.

Matters came to a head during a meeting in the Apple offices, when John kept turning down all of Paul's suggestions as to what the band should do next. The following year, John told *Rolling Stone* interviewer Jann Wenner, "So it came to a point I had to say something, of course, and Paul said, 'What do you mean?' I said, 'I mean the group is over, I'm leaving.'. . . Like anybody when you say divorce, you know, their face goes all sorts of colors. It's like he knew, really, this was the final thing."

The end for the Beatles meant the beginning of a new era for John, and the realization that, for the first time in his life, he didn't have to comply to what people wanted or expected of him. Yoko was all the support he needed but, in a musical sense, from here on in he would have to fall back pretty exclusively on his own talent. A completely new adventure was about to begin.

JOHN LENNON

CHAPTER 11

PEACE, LOVE AND POLITICS

"John and Yoko? Some people think they're mad, but he's only being John!"

RINGO STARR
1969
(*Disc* magazine)

Opposite: Following the break-up of the Beatles, John and Yoko became increasingly involved in what many observers considered radical politics. This shot of the Plastic Ono supergroup was snapped backstage at London's Lyceum Ballroom following a December 15, 1969, "Peace for Christmas" concert. At the far left of the second row, standing alongside the likes of Eric Clapton, Billy Preston, and Keith Moon, is George Harrison; this occasion was the first time he and John appeared on stage together since the summer of 1966.

March 20, 1969: John and Yoko in mid-flight, on their way back to Paris
after marrying in Gibraltar.

By anyone's standards, even John Lennon's, 1969 was a truly remarkable year. During the period when man first landed on the moon, when thousands of young men were dying in Vietnam, and nearly half a million kids gathered for a three-day rock concert near Woodstock in upstate New York, John's own life was packed with action, incident, drama, and controversy.

Never one to do things by halves, he not only threw himself with boundless energy and enthusiasm into everything that he and Yoko did, but he also ensured that all of this took place within the full glare of the media spotlight. This way, they both reasoned, they could gain maximum exposure for two of the things that mattered to them most: Their political views and their art, which were increasingly becoming one and the same thing.

During the early years of the Beatles' international fame, John had been under strict instruction from Brian Epstein to keep his opinions on subjects such as the Vietnam War to himself. As time went on, however, and as pro-peace movements around the world began to grow, he made his feelings clear to anyone who asked. Now he was going to give his opinions free rein.

The finalization of Yoko's divorce from her second husband, Tony Cox, in February 1969, along with the custody that she was granted of their daughter, Kyoko, opened the way for her and John to marry. This they did in Gibraltar on March 20. Five days later the newlyweds moved into Room 902 of the Hilton Hotel in Amsterdam, Holland, and embarked on a seven-day "bed-in" for peace.

JOHN LENNON

"We knew that whatever we did was going to be in the papers," John told Tom Snyder on NBC television's *Tomorrow* show in April 1975. "So we decided to utilize the space we would occupy anyway by getting married, with a commercial for peace and also a theatrical event. And the theatrical event we came up with, which utilized the least energy with the maximum effect, was to work from bed, and what we virtually had was a seven-day press conference in bed.

"The press, on the first day, they fought at the door to get in, thinking there was something, y'know, sexy going on, and they found two people talking about peace. And reporters always have five minutes with you or ten minutes with you; we let them ask anything for as long as they wanted for seven days, and all the time we just kept plugging peace."

The scene that was captured by the world's cameras was one of John and Yoko sitting in their pajamas on top of a large double bed, surrounded by friends, reporters, flowers, and hand-drawn posters exclaiming "Peace," "Hair Peace" (a typically Lennonish pun), "Remember Love," and "Bagism."

This last-mentioned term referred to the couple's recent tendency to give interviews while inside a large white bag. One of the most celebrated examples of this came immediately after the week-long spell in Amsterdam, when the Lennons flew to Austria in order to hold a press conference at Vienna's Hotel Sacher. With cameras whirring and clicking, and the reporters looking simultaneously confused and amused, John explained that they were witnessing another peace protest. "But why the bag?" asked one of the onlookers.

"Because we believe in total communication," came the reply from within. "That means if we have something to say, or anybody has something to say, they can communicate and not confuse you with what color your skin is or how long your hair's grown. . . .

"All we're saying is give peace a chance. But if the least we can do is give somebody a laugh, we're willing to be the world's clowns, because we think it's a bit serious at the moment and a bit intellectual."

May 1969: John meets Yoko's daughter, Kyoko, for the first time, after she has flown into London's Heathrow Airport from the United States. Smiles of joy for now, but tears and heartache would follow when the little girl's father, Anthony Cox, would eventually disappear with her for many years.

JOHN LENNON

Both pages: Scenes from a wedding. Yoko, John, and best man Peter Brown
listen attentively (*above*) to Registrar Cecil Wheeler during the ceremony in
Gibraltar, March 20, 1969. *Opposite:* Standing near the Rock of Gibraltar,
John proudly holds aloft the prized wedding certificate. "Intellectually,
we didn't believe in getting married," he said. "But one doesn't love
someone just intellectually."

JOHN LENNON

JOHN LENNON

Room 902 of the Hilton Hotel in Amsterdam, Holland becomes the focus
of worldwide media attention when John and Yoko hold their first bed-in for
peace on March 25-31, 1969.

Opposite: "It's a love that lasts forever, It's a love that has no past."

Many people certainly did view John and Yoko as clowns. At the same time that images of the bedded and bagged couple appeared in newspapers and cartoons around the globe, their names were dropped into the middle of a gag by every two-bit comedian who wanted an easy laugh.

But for all this, what John had said was absolutely correct: Intellectual discussions on the subject of promoting peace rarely made the front pages of national papers and magazines, whereas the antics of himself and Yoko undeniably did. One way or the other, they were getting their message across and making people smile at the same time. Their credibility may have been suffering, but it was difficult to criticize their sentiments.

The main reason for John and Yoko's visit to Austria, in fact, was to promote *Rape,* a new avant-garde film that they had produced. The movie sets out to demonstrate how the media often make unfair intrusions into people's lives; it does this by having a cameraman and sound assistant pick out an innocent girl walking in Central London, and then follow her wherever she goes. Initially amused, she eventually becomes angry, frightened, and confused, especially when the two movie-men follow her home.

Rape was, indeed, one of the more easy to understand of John and Yoko's cinematic efforts. Having involved Yoko in his music and taken part in her art exhibitions, John was also interested in participating in her particular brand of film-

JOHN LENNON

JOHN LENNON

"And in the end. . . ." One of the last shots
of the Beatles together. Tittenhurst Park,
August 1969.

making. Yoko's specialty was to capture a piece of action – no matter how brief – with a high-speed camera and then replay the footage in super-slow motion. So it was that between 1968 and 1972 their movie collaborations included *Smile,* a 52-minute film of John smiling, raising his eyebrows, and sticking his tongue out; *Self-Portrait,* a 15-minute close-up of John's penis; and *Erection,* a study not of John, but of the 18-month construction of the London International Hotel, accelerated in this case to 18 minutes. In *Up Your Legs Forever,* 331 people were filmed from foot to thigh.

Some of the work, as simplistic as it may have appeared, did have a loose structure: *Two Virgins,* for instance, consisted of 19 minutes' worth of John and Yoko's faces superimposing and eventually merging.

Many of the pair's other film projects, however, were in the Andy Warhol let's-shoot-and-see-what-happens tradition, whereby a camera would be turned on and left to capture whatever might take place. Therefore, 18 continuous minutes of a flight in a helium balloon were the sum total of *Apotheosis,* while the unforgettable *Fly* featured a little winged wonder crawling his way around the nooks and crannies of a naked woman's body.

All of this was clearly a million miles away from the likes of *A Hard Day's Night* and *Help!;* for John these films were not merely illustrative of his new interests, but evidence that he had dedicated himself to starting a brand new life. In later years he would refer to the 1940-1968 period before he teamed up with Yoko as "my first incarnation." In line with this way of thinking, on April 22, 1969 he changed his middle name from Winston to Ono in a formal ceremony on the roof of the Beatles' Apple building. From now on, therefore, he would call himself John Ono Lennon.

The previous year's drug conviction came back to haunt John in May, when the U.S. authorities refused to grant him a visitor's visa. Regardless, he and Yoko wanted to carry their message of love and peace to the Americans, so they held their second bed-in at the Queen Elizabeth Hotel in Montreal,

Yoko, Kyoko, and John: the temporary family, 1969. When John and Yoko
would leave the U.K. for the U.S. in September of 1971, the initial purpose
of their trip would be to track down Yoko's little girl.

JOHN LENNON

Symbolic of his love for Yoko and the peace activities the couple were pursuing,
John often attended the 1969 *Let It Be* sessions dressed entirely in white.

JOHN LENNON

Surrounded by flowers, press men, and hangers-on, John and Yoko record the anthem, "Give Peace a Chance" in Montreal on June 1, 1969. Note John's portraits of himself and his wife on his guitar.

Canada. Here it was, in Room 1742, that on June 1 they recorded their classic anthem, "Give Peace a Chance," together with the many visitors who were gathered around their bed.

A couple of years earlier, John had told the world that no problem was too great because, in the end, "All you need is love." Yet many people still seemed intent on waging war, even if it didn't really get them anywhere. How about trying something else for a change? "All we are saying is give peace a chance," was the simple yet powerful suggestion, and one that filtered through to all corners of the globe.

Although this song was credited to Lennon-McCartney, it was, in fact, the first single release from The Plastic Ono Band. This was the name given by John and Yoko to a variety of musicians who backed them both in concert and on record,

including a lineup that featured Eric Clapton on lead guitar, Klaus Voorman on bass, and Alan White on drums; it was this ensemble that was heard on the chilling "Cold Turkey" single released later in the year. A document of the painful symptoms of withdrawal from heroin addiction, the record boasted one of John's most extraordinary vocal performances to date, alternately trembling and hysterical, as he pleaded:

> "Oh, I'll be a good boy,
> Please make me well,
> I'll promise you anything,
> Get me out of this hell."

While he was giving less and less of his time to the Beatles, John nevertheless still contributed some memorable numbers to the group's final efforts. Many of these were Yoko-inspired,

Ringo (left) with the Lennons and McCartneys at Paul and Linda's
London home, April 1969.

such as "Don't Let Me Down" from *Let It Be,* and "The Ballad Of John And Yoko," the group's final #1 single in the United Kingdom.

On the *Abbey Road* album, three of the songs illustrated the ways in which John would vary his techniques as a composer: After listening to Yoko playing Beethoven's "Moonlight Sonata" on the piano, he reversed the chords, wrote some lyrics, and came up with "Because"; indulging his passion for wordplay and nonsense poetry, he wrote "Come Together," a sort of Son of I Am The Walrus; and then, reverting to the other extreme, the seven-minute, 46-second "I Want You (She's So Heavy)" mainly consisted of John singing:

> "I want you.
> I want you so bad, babe.
> I want you.
> I want you so bad,
> it's driving me mad.
> It's driving me mad."

After a reviewer commented that these lyrics showed that the composer had lost his creative talent, John explained to *Rolling Stone* interviewer Jann Wenner that they were simple in order to make his message clear. "When you're drowning you don't say, 'I would be incredibly pleased if someone would have the foresight to notice me drowning and come and help me.' You just scream!"

True enough, but the activities of the Lennons during this period were not quite so straightforward. A car crash while vacationing with Julian and Kyoko in Scotland was followed in September by a live appearance with The Plastic Ono Band at a rock 'n' roll festival in Toronto. Yoko suffered another miscarriage in October, but she was sufficiently recovered by December to continue with her husband on two of their campaigns: To clear the name of James Hanratty, one of the last men to have been hanged in Britain, and to promote peace around the world by having huge billboards erected in eleven different cities, proclaiming "War Is Over! If You Want It. Happy Christmas from John & Yoko."

Following a crash into a ditch while on vacation in Scotland in July 1969, John and Yoko pose in front of their wrecked Austin Maxi. They later had the car placed on a concrete pedestal in the grounds of their home at Tittenhurst Park.

JOHN LENNON

In the midst of a great deal of feverish musical and political activity, John and
Yoko faced the responsibility of maintaining a loving relationship
with John's young son, Julian.

Two days before Christmas, 1969, John increased his standing as a "man of the people" when he and Yoko had a 51-minute private meeting with the Canadian Prime Minister, Pierre Trudeau. Afterwards, a beaming John told the assembled press men, "If there were more leaders like Mr. Trudeau, the world would have peace. . . . You don't know how lucky you are in Canada."

Associating with a major political figure could only do good for John's cause. Yet he hadn't exactly endeared himself to the authorities in Britain a month earlier, when he put into action a plan that had been brewing in his head for quite some time: He returned his MBE medal to the Queen! Never at ease with the honor, he had been searching for reasons to return the award ever since receiving it, and on November 25, 1969 he came up with three:

"Your Majesty," read the letter that had been typed on Bag Productions note paper, "I am returning this M.B.E. in protest against Britain's involvement in the Nigeria-Biafra thing, against

our support of America in Vietnam, and against 'Cold Turkey' slipping down the charts. With Love, John Lennon of Bag."

The reference to his record was John's way of injecting some humor into the situation, but of course not everyone chose to see it this way. Writer Anthony Fawcett, in his book, *John Lennon One Day at a Time,* recounted what happened next: "I don't think the Queen will be embarrassed," said John. "The Queen is above embarrassment," came the formal reply from Buckingham Palace.

More trouble with an unsmiling Establishment came in January of 1970, when police raided the London Arts Gallery, where 14 of John's lithographs – drawings depicting various aspects of his and Yoko's marriage and honeymoon – were on exhibit. Eight of these drawings were adjudged to be indecent, and were confiscated by the men from Scotland Yard, only to be cleared in a court case and returned a few months later.

Meanwhile, both John and Yoko had their hair cropped, pronounced 1970 as "Year One for Peace," and released the excellent "Instant Karma! (We All Shine On)" single, which had been written, recorded, and mixed by John in just one day. "I wrote it for breakfast, recorded it for lunch, and we're putting it out for dinner," he told a reporter at the time.

On April Fools' Day 1970 John and Yoko issued a fictitious press statement, announcing that the pair had entered the London Clinic in order to have his 'n' hers sex-change operations! They knew that at this stage of the game some people would believe they were capable of doing anything. They enjoyed the stir that their little hoax created but privately, however, they were going through a very difficult time.

The strain of their intense activity, together with the kidnapping of Yoko's seven-year-old daughter by her ex-husband, was beginning to take its toll. On April 23 the Lennons flew to Los Angeles in order to undergo a four-month psychiatric course under Dr. Arthur Janov. He had designed a form of treatment called Primal Therapy, in which the patient is encouraged to recall many of his or her most painful experiences, going all the way back to early childhood, and then attempt to come to terms with these by letting out a loud scream in order to relieve the tension; a "primal scream."

John began to face up to many of his lifelong insecurities: his father's desertion, his mother's death, and his image of himself. The result was that on returning to England he produced a masterwork based on these subjects; his first proper studio album as a solo artist, entitled simply *John Lennon/Plastic Ono Band*.

With only guitar, bass, drums, and occasional contributions from a piano, the sound was harsh, basic rock 'n' roll, highlighted by John's brutally honest lyrics about his parents' neglect ("Mother" and "My Mummy's Dead"), the trials of growing up and facing rejection ("Working Class Hero"), the shallowness of fame ("Isolation," "God," and "I Found Out"), and his hope for the future ("Love," "Hold On," and "Look At Me"). John is talking directly to the listener, taking him or her into his confidence, and offering advice based on his own experiences. In "Working Class Hero" he sings:

John returned his MBE to the Queen on November 25, 1969. Although he softened the gesture with a bit of Lennon-style humor, the act was perceived by many Britons as an affront to the whole nation. In the photo above, taken at John and Yoko's Apple office following the medal's return, John looks nearly as stunned as the public.

JOHN LENNON

Back at Tittenhurst after a trip to Denmark, John and Yoko declare 1970 to be "Year One for Peace." Missing the point entirely, the *Daily Mirror* labels their haircuts "the most sensational scalpings since the Red Indians went out of business."

"They hurt you at home
and they hit you at school,
They hate you if you're clever
and they despise a fool,
'Til you're so f_____ crazy
you can't follow their rules."

And in "I Found Out" he states bitterly:

"I seen through junkies,
I been through it all.
I seen religion
from Jesus to Paul,
Don't let them fool you
with dope and cocaine,
No one can harm you,
feel your own pain."

Face up to your problems, is the basic message, without resorting to drugs or man-made philosophies as a crutch. In "God," John then carries this line of reasoning a step further by running off a whole list of political, religious, and popular leaders and ideas – including the Beatles – in which he doesn't believe, before stating that reality for him is his future with Yoko. He also set the record straight about his former group:

"I was the dream-weaver,
but now I'm reborn;
I was the walrus,
but now I am John.
And so dear friends,
you'll just have to carry on.
The dream is over."

Critic Greil Marcus once described John's singing of this particular passage as "possibly the finest in all of rock music"; it was certainly one of the most beautiful vocal performances that John ever recorded. The lyrics, for their part, left little to the imagination, and all in all this was pretty dramatic stuff.

Hitching a ride, Julian Lennon has good reason for looking slightly skeptical . . .
his dad is driving!

Having appeared physically naked on the cover of *Two Virgins,* John was now presenting himself emotionally naked. In the hands of a lesser artist this could – and, most probably, would – have ended up being completely embarrassing, especially considering the sound of John's near-hysteria when he howled out some of the more personally painful lines, such as "Mama don't go, Daddy come home," at the end of "Mother."

Not many recording artists could have gotten away with work of such a personal nature, but John's talent and basic integrity allowed him to pull it off. In the process he single-handedly advanced the art of popular music as a means of communication. This was yet another high point in his career, and the following year, 1971, he continued the trend with the *Imagine* album.

Again, almost every track was quite outstanding, but this time around the music was, for the most part, gentler and more melodic, as John sang with greater calm about his insecurities ("Crippled Inside," "Jealous Guy," "It's So Hard,"

"I Don't Want To Be A Soldier," and "How?"), his beliefs ("Give Me Some Truth" and the title-track), and his personal happiness ("Oh My Love" and "Oh Yoko!").

In sharp contrast to the introspection, however, was "How Do You Sleep?," a song full of sarcastic insults aimed directly at Paul McCartney, in response to what John had perceived as some less-than-complimentary remarks in the recent work of his ex-friend and partner. But whereas few people would have been aware of Paul's typically subtle jibes, there could be little mistaking what John was trying to say:

"You live with straights
who tell you, you was king,
Jump when your momma
tell you anything,
The only thing
you done was yesterday,
And since you've gone
you're just another day."

Their cropped hair symbolic of their commitment to world peace, John and
Yoko share a reflective moment. The press, eager to deride them,
happily painted the couple as eccentrics, but John and Yoko's
motivations were nothing if not sincere.

The song's mention of "momma" was a mischievous reference to Paul's wife, Linda, and the allusion to "Yesterday" suggests John's opinion that the popular Beatles hit was Paul's only composition of real distinction. "Another Day" was the title of one of the pair's recent singles. Still, just in case anyone missed the point, while the cover shot of Paul's *Ram* album featured him holding onto one of his woolly friends on his Scottish farm, John's *Imagine* LP came with a free photo of Mr. Lennon grappling with a pig!

This, of course, was simply a case of John showing his snippy side and illustrating, as he would have been the first to admit, that he had faults and weaknesses like anyone else.

"There was something very spiritual and magical about John," recalls record producer Eddy Offord, who engineered three of the tracks on the *Imagine* album. "He was such a simple kind of guy – very down-to-earth – but he had a feeling that was very special, and I will never ever forget that experience. . . . When I look back on my career, it was, actually, one of the highlights."

Honesty being one of his main virtues, there could be no doubting the sincerity of the sentiments that John expressed in two other songs from this period, both of which are now rightly regarded as classics. On the single "Happy Xmas (War is Over)," he once again preached peace and harmony among all people:

"And so happy Xmas,
For black and for white,
For the yellow and red ones,
Let's stop all the fight."

John performs "Instant Karma!" on British television's *Top of the Pops* in
February 1970. He and Yoko had declared 1970 "Year One for Peace," and
followed through on the sentiment in numerous recordings released in 1970-71.

JOHN LENNON

This page: John and Yoko make music and just relax at their Tittenhurst Park home, 1971. John's box guitar (*below, left*) was custom-made.

JOHN LENNON

Tittenhurst Park, Sunninghill, Berkshire. The estate was purchased by John and
Yoko in May of 1969; the *Imagine* album was recorded here.
Ringo bought the property in 1973 and sold it in 1990.

The *Imagine* title track, on the other hand, pictured a world without all of the things that have caused heartache, pain and suffering, since the start of time; no fighting over beliefs, no greed, no starvation.

> "Imagine there's no countries.
> It isn't hard to do.
> Nothing to kill or die for,
> and no religion, too.
> Imagine all the people
> sharing all the world. . . ."

Lyrics such as these best sum up John's heartfelt hopes and desires, yet he and Yoko were still suffering the intolerance of a British public which had never taken to her. The four-month stay in Los Angeles the previous year had provided a different experience, with people more willing to accept the couple on their own terms, while also allowing them the freedom to walk the streets along with everyone else. America appeared fresh and exciting; the place of John's dreams, the country that had given birth to rock 'n' roll.

"I should have been born in New York," he told *Rolling Stone* magazine's Jann Wenner at the time. "I should have been born in the [Greenwich] Village, that's where I belong. . . . Everybody heads towards the center, that's why I'm here now. I'm here just to breathe it."

Back in England, the Lennons had moved to the Ascot countryside in order to escape from prying eyes, but although their Tittenhurst Park mansion was certainly magnificent – set in 70 acres of beautiful heathland and woods, complete with an artificial lake – John and Yoko felt isolated there.

On September 3, 1971, they left London's Heathrow Airport for New York. Initially, this was to be a short visit aimed at locating Yoko's daughter, Kyoko; but John, although he didn't realize it at the time, would never see his native country again.

JOHN LENNON

CHAPTER 12

THE LOST
WEEKEND

*"It was a year or two of just
getting it out there....
[John] was over twenty-one,
he got drunk, he couldn't
handle it and he got a little
crazier than most."*

HARRY NILSSON
1982
(*The Ballad of John and Yoko* by the Editors of *Rolling Stone*)

Opposite: Political pressures, the threat of deportation, and innate restlessness
helped to precipitate John's 1973-75 estrangement from Yoko. Suddenly free of
domestic responsibility, John gave himself over to self-indulgent behavior that
sorely tested his mind and body, and put his marriage in peril.

John and Yoko's political activity led to the famous 1970 hair-cropping on behalf
of radical black leader Michael X. This and similar activities eventually
captured the attention of the United States government,
which perceived John and Yoko as a threat to national security.

During early 1971, a noticeable shift of emphasis took place in the political beliefs of John and Yoko. Until now, they had preached non-violence at all costs, sending acorns to world leaders as a symbol of their peace campaign, and urging students caught up in the notorious Berkeley riots of 1969 not to retaliate when provoked by the authorities.

On the song "Revolution," which was the B-side to the Beatles' 1968 "Hey Jude" single, John had sung:

"You say you want a revolution
Well, you know,
we all want to change the world"

If others wanted to rebel against law and order to bring about a complete change within society, then that was up to them, but he wasn't yet sure whether or not he wanted to become involved in these activities. By March of '71, however, when the single, "Power To The People," was released, the Lennons were posing for publicity photos decked out in Japanese riot gear, and John was singing:

"Say we want a revolution
We better get it on right away
Well you get on your feet
And into the street"

Clearly, they were now ready to take up the cause (whatever that might happen to be), but they were walking on slippery ground. They should have learned their lesson from an embarrassing episode that had taken place the previous year, when they had their hair cropped and donated the trimmings to the notorious British Black Power leader, Michael X (real name: Michael Abdul Malik). He in turn auctioned the trimmings and used the proceeds to support a black-culture center in London. John and Yoko were happy to pose for photos with him, but they must have been dismayed a few months later when X's "Black House" burned down and he was arrested for robbery. In 1973, X would be convicted in Trinidad of committing two murders, and, despite John paying for his appeals, he would be hanged in 1975.

John had freed himself from being a Beatle, yet he seemed unable to keep away from those who were only too happy to latch onto him and profit from his status as an ex-Beatle. This was especially true once he and Yoko had moved to New York. Basing themselves after a few months in a two-room apartment at 155 Bank Street in the West Village, they were soon surrounded by all manner of political radicals, including Abbie Hoffman, "Yippie" leader Jerry Rubin, rock "activist" David Peel, and Black Panther chairman Bobby Seale.

The bottom line of these people's shared interest was to help bring about the overthrow of President Nixon's government, and discussions would go on late into the night at the Bank Street address in which the participants devised ways in which to achieve their aim. Out of this came the Lennons' involvement in protest rallies, several concerts in benefit of some worthy and not-so-worthy causes, and the most disappointing studio album of John's career.

Some Time In New York City, released in the United States in June of 1972, boasted a cover that mimicked the look of a typical *New York Times* front page, complete with song lyrics printed to look like feature stories, and accompanying photos that included a mocked-up shot of Nixon and China's Chairman Mao dancing naked together. Inside there were two records, and while the second one comprised live material from a couple of John and Yoko's concert appearances, the body of new work was contained on the first disc.

These new songs, some written by both John and Yoko, others separate efforts, stated the cases of different social and political issues that had been brought to their attention:

John loved New York City, and appreciated its excitement and vigor. Abbie Hoffman, Jerry Rubin, and other high-profile political activists were part of that excitement, and led John and Yoko into a more strident sort of activism.

April 22, 1972: John and Yoko address the crowd at a National Peace Rally in Bryanston Park, New York. Their appearance coincided with ongoing deportation hearings at the city's U.S. Immigration and Naturalization Office.

Northern Ireland, Women's Liberation, the imprisonment of left-wing radicals John Sinclair and Angela Davis, and the Attica State Prison shootings. The idea of presenting the album almost like a collection of journalists' reports wasn't a bad one, but the problem was that the readers – or, in this case, the listeners – found it difficult to believe that John and Yoko had a passionate concern for what seemed to be every cause that came their way.

Reinforcing the fans' dubious perception of the LP were John's lyrics, which were unusually awkward and often pieced together expressly to make a political point. This was the case even with a strong track like "Woman is the Nigger of the World":

> "We make her bear
> and raise our children
> And then we leave her flat
> for being a fat old mother hen
> We tell her home
> is the only place she should be
> Then we complain
> that she's too unworldly
> to be our friend"

Not John at his best; he seemed merely to be reflecting other people's opinions, rather than describing feelings that came from his own heart. Dealing in areas that were unfamiliar

By 1972, John and Yoko seemed to be championing just about every social or
political cause that came their way. In this case, it happens to be
the plight of Native Americans.

to him, he was, quite simply, out of his range.

In Britain, where the record was released in September of the same year, the public didn't take kindly to being labeled a bunch of brutal murderers in songs such as "The Luck Of The Irish" and "Sunday Bloody Sunday," especially since those sentiments came from someone who shared their nationality but had moved away from their national problems.

"Why the hell are the English there anyway
As they kill with God on their side!
Blame it all on the kids and the IRA
As the bastards commit genocide"

In the U.S., meanwhile, the government was keeping strict tabs on "Mr. Lennon." Earlier in 1972, he and Yoko had been served with deportation orders on the grounds of John's 1968 cannabis conviction, but what he didn't realize at the time was that the moves to oust him were being directed by the top man in the land. President Nixon had been informed by his advisors that John had fallen in with bad company, people who would stop at nothing to undermine the Republican Party's chances of winning the forthcoming election. With the public backing of an ex-Beatle, the members of this anti-Nixon faction were evolving from being a nuisance into a major threat.

Memos and reports flew back and forth between senators, the FBI, and the U.S. immigration office, all revolving around the paranoid order to "get Lennon out." At first, John thought he was only imagining that his phone was being tapped and that he was being followed by cars, but pretty soon he began to get the message.

Every time he was ordered out of the country his lawyer would delay the process and file an appeal. Public figures came forward to support him, including New York City's Mayor Lindsay, but all of this was ignored by the authorities, who had been "reliably informed" that John and his radical colleagues were planning to disrupt the Republican National Convention in San Diego that August.

In actual fact, the authorities had been misinformed. When Rubin, Hoffman and Co. revealed that they were planning to cause a riot, John and Yoko lost interest in the group's activities and backed away. Raising fists in the air was one thing, but using them to hurt innocent people was unacceptable.

"We said, 'We ain't buying this,'" John told *Playboy* interviewer David Sheff in 1980. "'We're not going to draw children into a situation to create violence – so you can overthrow what? And replace it with what?'. . . It was all based on this illusion, that you can create violence and overthrow what is, and get communism or get some right-wing lunatic or a left-wing lunatic. They're all lunatics."

In a 1980 interview with *Newsweek's* Barbara Graustark, he would admit that his political activism of the early '70s had been misguided, basically stemming from a feeling of guilt over earning so much money. "When you stop and think, what the hell was I doing fighting the American government just because Jerry Rubin couldn't get what he always wanted – a nice, cushy job."

Their radical days virtually at an end, John and Yoko now reverted to more constructive ways of trying to right the world's wrongs. On August 30, they headlined two *One to One* concerts at New York's Madison Square Garden, raising $1.5 million for retarded people and personally donating $60,000 in the process. Although John would appear on stage a couple of more times during the next few years, these were

John slays the Madison Square Garden crowds with his no-nonsense rock approach, while headlining two "One to One" charity concerts with Yoko at the New York venue, on August 30, 1972. Backed by Elephant's Memory and supported by an all-star ensemble including Sha-Na-Na, Roberta Flack, Stevie Wonder, and Phil Spector, the couple managed to raise $1.5 million to aid retarded people. On their own, John and Yoko donated $60,000.

to be his last full-scale shows.

December 1972 saw the release of the *Imagine* film, based on the 1971 album of the same name, and featuring the couple at work and at play, both in Ascot and New York. By 1973, however, their relationship was not quite so harmonious. The pressures of John's immigration problems, Yoko's unsuccessful search for her daughter, their disappointment with their political activities, the negative response to their recent recordings – all of these caused cracks in the marriage.

Any such problems were not apparent on John's *Mind Games* album, however, which was released in November. Musically, it seemed to be a purposeful return to the familiar themes of peace, freedom, and John's love for Yoko, all of which had characterized the music he had produced a couple years before. It also meant that John was at least now facing in the right direction again, even though, for the first time in his career, he had to take a backward step in order to achieve this.

By no means a classic piece of work, *Mind Games* did have some great moments, such as the powerful title track, the Latinesque "You Are Here," and the beautiful love song, "Out the Blue," in which John sings:

With Yoko assisting, John indulges his talent for drawing, as well as his passion for sick humor. Note the blind man roller skating, together with the guide dog wearing sunglasses!

> "All my life has been
> a long slow knife
> I was born just to get to you
> Anyway, I survived
> long enough
> to make you my wife"

Heartfelt sentiments indeed, yet by the time these words were being broadcast on the radio and played on people's stereo systems, John and Yoko were no longer living together. He had moved to Los Angeles with his wife's former secretary, an attractive Asian girl named May Pang. Later, conflicting accounts would attempt to explain how this change in lifestyle came about. May's opinion was that John had left of his own free will; John, on the other hand, asserted to Andy Peebles

March 12, 1974, at L.A.'s Troubadour Club, just before things got out of hand.
John and Harry Nilsson—with May Pang sitting between them—knock back
Brandy Alexanders; an amused Peter Lawford watches.

during the BBC radio interview that Yoko, sick of his irritable moods and fading concern for her, "said 'Get the hell out' and kicked me out."

Either way, it was decided that the trustworthy Miss Pang would be a good companion for John during the trial separation; his initial reaction was relief at his new-found freedom. For the first time since he was at Art College, he was virtually unattached.

As John recounted to *Playboy's* David Sheff, "Well, first I thought, 'Whoopee! Bachelor life! Whoopee, whoopee!' And then I woke up one day and thought, 'What is this? I want to go home.' But she [Yoko] wouldn't let me come home. . . . We were talking all the time on the phone and I kept saying, 'I don't like this. I'm out of control. I'm drinking. I'm getting into trouble and I'd like to come home, please.' And she's saying, 'You're not ready to come home.' 'What are you saying?' Well, okay, back to the bottle."

Drowning his sorrows at the bar, John chose as his drinking buddies some of the recording industry's most seasoned tipplers, including Ringo, Keith Moon, and Harry Nilsson. Living together at a Santa Monica beach house, they caused all sorts of mayhem, and John, always at his most offensive when under the influence of alcohol, got himself both into trouble and into the newspapers.

One of the most notorious incidents took place at L.A.'s Troubadour Club in March of 1974, when John and Harry heckled the Smothers Brothers during their stage act and, after allegedly assaulting the brothers' manager and a waitress, were thrown out onto the street.

For John, this sort of behavior was all too reminiscent of his Art College days, the only difference being that he was now in his mid-thirties and well aware of how damaging the alcohol was to him – physically, mentally, and publicly.

He later reflected to interviewer David Sheff, "If I died –

Not all of John's time in L.A. was hectic. While relaxing in late 1973 at the
Bel-Air home of producer Lou Adler, John read and quietly made music.

Despite his relationship with May Pang, John kept in touch with Yoko. Still, his
choice of music (*above, right*), seems ironic.

JOHN LENNON

"Go Johnny go, go. . . ." Jamming with his teenage idol, Chuck Berry, on the February 16, 1972, broadcast of *The Mike Douglas Show;* John and Yoko co-hosted five consecutive shows with Douglas. For John, the opportunity to play with Berry was a dream come true.

Opposite: Producer Phil Spector, shown here listening to playback with John during the *Imagine* album sessions in 1971, got together with John a few years later to record an oldies album. A notoriously egocentric perfectionist, Spector had had his first recording success in the late 1950s, while still a teenager. By the early sixties, he had practically created the "girl group" sound via the Ronettes, the Crystals, and other artists. An oldies collaboration with John probably seemed like an inspired idea, but Spector's eccentricities—coupled with John's unrestrained lifestyle—spelled disaster.

the way [poet] Dylan Thomas died – they'd be saying, 'What a wonderful, colorful way to go.' Because I'm alive, it's not so wonderful. It was the worst time of my life."

Recording sessions aimed at putting together a collection of rock 'n' roll oldies with legendary – and legendarily eccentric – producer Phil Spector also fell apart under the spell of brandy and brawling. Spector, himself not exactly noted for his restraint, subsequently complicated matters by mysteriously disappearing with the master tapes after being involved in a car crash.

John's original intention had been to put together an album of some of his favorite songs, without having to worry about writing the material or even producing and arranging it. Now he was beginning to regret this decision, even though much of what Spector had in his possession was not of great commercial value anyway.

"There were 28 guys playing a night, and 15 of them were out of their minds, including me," John told Bob Harris in an interview for BBC Television's *The Old Grey Whistle Test* in 1975. "There were about eight tracks, half of them you couldn't use for one reason or another. . . . You've got 10 people playing out of tune."

While remaining in L.A. in a vain attempt to sort this situation out, John somehow managed to produce Nilsson's *Pussy Cats* album, even though the work was once again often undermined by booze. As if that weren't obstacle enough, Nilsson was suffering from a ruptured vocal cord!

"I was just hanging out with guys, and all we were doing was getting drunk and waking up," John told Bob Harris. "It was sick. . . . That's when I straightened out, in the middle of that [*Pussy Cats*] album. That's when I realized, 'There's something wrong here. Y'know, this is crazy, man!' So then I suddenly was the straight one in the middle of all these mad, mad people. I suddenly was not one of them, and I pulled myself back and finished off the album as best I could."

Making his way back to New York in June of 1974, John began to take some positive steps with regard to his own

JOHN LENNON

Despite the upset of his personal life in the early seventies, John maintained his
keen sense of humor and essential love of life. Then came the *Walls and
Bridges* album, which confirmed that his talent had not deserted him.

career. With the Phil Spector rock 'n' roll tracks still on ice, he wrote an astounding ten songs in the space of just one week and quickly recorded the *Walls and Bridges* album. Full of beautiful melodies and poetic, meaningful lyrics, this record signaled a definite return to form, and also served notice to May Pang that she didn't really fill the void left by Yoko.

May, who was the LP's production coordinator, was quick to pick up on the one track written with her in mind – "Surprise, Surprise (Sweet Bird of Paradox)" – but it was also difficult to miss the point of the other songs, most of which described John's feelings of loneliness and despair, and his continuing affection for his wife.

In "Bless You" he wrote:

> "Some people say it's over
> Now that we spread our wings
> But we know better darling
> The hollow ring is only last year's echo"

And in "Scared" he expressed his loneliness, his fear that he was wasting his life, and his awareness of the bad influences surrounding him:

> "Hatred and jealousy
> gonna be the death of me
> I guess I knew it
> right from the start
> Sing out about love and peace
> Don't wanna see the red raw meat
> The green eyed goddamn
> straight from your heart"

The album's finest moment, however, came with "Nobody Loves You (When You're Down and Out)," the only song that John composed on his own during the unhappy months in Los Angeles; it perfectly captured his feelings of depression:

> "I've been across the water now
> so many times
> I've seen the one-eyed witch doctor
> leading the blind
> And still you ask me do I love you
> what you say, what you say
> Everytime I put my finger on it
> it slips away"

Yet for all the heartache, one thing that never deserted John was his tremendous sense of humor. Throughout his life, this attribute helped him cope with even the most difficult situations. He had ample opportunity to display his wit during the promotion of the *Walls and Bridges* album, when he made live broadcasts on a number of radio stations.

One such occasion was his appearance on New York's WNEW-FM, when he sat in on Dennis Elsas's afternoon show on Saturday, September 28, 1974. Introducing himself to the listeners as "Dr. Winston O'Boogie," John was clearly in top form as he spoke to Elsas about his career past and present, and announced some of the commercials:

December 1974, and John settles in between girlfriend May Pang and son Julian during a New Year's vacation at Disney World in Florida. The arrangement would not last, however; the following month John would reunite with Yoko.

Two survivors of the "British Invasion," John and Mick Jagger, meet at a 1974
American Film Institute dinner in honor of James Cagney.

"Tonight, at the Joint in the Woods – guess who's there! – it's Ladies' Night! . . . All females admitted at half-price. Oh, good! Well, Bowie can get in! . . . Coming next Wednesday night at the Joint in the Woods – 'There's nothing like a joint in the woods,' said he, losing his Green Card [U.S. visa] possibilities in one blow! – T Rex!"

Then there were the weather forecasts: "We're not going to bother with the weather, just look out of the window! Oh, you want the weather? The degrees have changed. . . . Oh, this is a nice degree: The temperature is 69! . . . The weather in Central Park is still there. . . . Tomorrow will be just the same as today, only different," and on and on!

John's love of double meaning – both sexual and otherwise – came in handy the following week, when he turned up as a guest deejay on the breakfast show of KHJ radio in Los Angeles. This time around he was able to spin many of his favorite

records, field live phone-in questions from fans, and read commercials in mock accents suggestive of a variety of nationalities and sexual orientations. Not surprisingly, the station's ratings climbed to a new high, while the advertisers were happy to reach more listeners than they had paid for.

On an equally upbeat note, the two hit singles from *Walls and Bridges* were both bright, cheery numbers: the fantasy-like "#9 Dream" and the catchy "Whatever Gets You Thru the Night," which featured Elton John on keyboards and harmony vocal. John returned the compliment by playing and singing on Elton's cover versions of "Lucy In The Sky With Diamonds" and "One Day (At A Time)." Almost as a joke, Elton asked John if he would join him on stage in the event that "Whatever Gets You Thru the Night" topped the American charts. John, who hadn't yet had a solo #1 single in the States and didn't imagine he was about to get one, casually agreed.

Madison Square Garden, November 28, 1974: John keeps a promise and joins
Elton John on stage. Yoko is in the audience, and after the show
the estranged couple meet backstage for the first time in months.

He was totally amazed, therefore, when the song hit the top of the *Billboard* charts on November 16, but on the 28th he kept his promise when he fought back an attack of nerves and walked on stage at New York's Madison Square Garden during Elton's Thanksgiving Day concert there. The crowd, which had heard rumors about a possible appearance by the ex-Beatle, nearly raised the roof when he strode out sporting long center-parted hair, a black cape, and dark, round glasses. The excitement continued as the two stars launched into full-blooded versions of the songs which they had recently recorded together. John then stepped up to the mike and announced, "I'd like to thank Elton and the boys for having me on tonight. We tried to think of a number to finish off with, so that I could get out of here and be sick . . . And we thought we'd do a number of an old estranged fiancé of mine called Paul. This is one I never sang, it's an old Beatle number,

and we just about know it."

The song was "I Saw Her Standing There," and the first chords were all the cue the fans needed to go absolutely wild. Sitting among them that night was Yoko; accounts differ as to whether John did or didn't know she was there. Either way, when they met backstage afterwards, the moment was nearly as intense as when they first made eye contact back at the Indica Gallery in 1966. The reconciliation had happened at last and by January 1975 they were living together once more. As John commented in a French television interview a few months later, "Our separation was a failure."

Hereafter, he would refer to the period spent apart from Yoko as his "Lost Weekend." (In actual fact, it had lasted about 15 months.) Having turned the final page of yet another chapter in his life, John was once again prepared to put the past behind him and start anew.

CHAPTER 13

BORROWED TIME

*"I would sit around
thinking, 'What does this
remind me of? . . . This
reminds me of being fifteen.'
I didn't have to write songs
at fifteen. I wrote if I wanted
to, or I played rock 'n' roll
if I wanted to."*

JOHN LENNON
1980
(BBC interview with John and Yoko, conducted by Andy Peebles)

Opposite: Performing "Slippin' and Slidin'" and "Imagine," John takes part in
Salute to Lew Grade, a television special recorded on April 18, 1975 and
broadcast in the United States on June 13. Nobody knew it at the time,
but after more than 1,400 live performances during 18 years,
this would be John's last-ever stage appearance.

Ending as he had begun: The cover of the 34-year-old superstar's last album before his temporary retirement depicted him as a 20-year-old rocker in Hamburg. On the back of the record's sleeve, John fondly asserted, "You should have been there."

In his 1980 interview with the BBC's Andy Peebles, John commented, "At the end of *Rock 'n' Roll,* on a track called "Just Because" . . . you hear me saying, 'And so we say farewell from Record Plant' . . . and something flashed through me mind as I said it; am I really saying farewell to the business? It wasn't conscious and it was a long, long time before I did take time out. And I looked at the cover which I'd chosen, which was a picture of me in Hamburg the first time [the Beatles] got there. . . . Here I am with this old picture of me in Hamburg in '61, and I'm saying farewell from Record Plant, and I'm ending as I started, singing this straight rock 'n' roll stuff."

What John was referring to was the spoken bridge near the end of "Just Because," in which he says: "This is Dr. Winston O'Boogie, saying goodnight from Record Plant East, New York. We hope you had a swell time, everybody here says 'Hi!' . . . Goodbye." This passage had been overdubbed in New York, even though the song itself was one of the few recordings done in Los Angeles with Phil Spector that finally made it onto the long overdue *Rock 'n' Roll* album.

After Spector had eventually returned the tapes to John and John had listened to them, he decided that if the record was to be salvaged then most of the out-of-tune material from 1973 would have to be re-recorded. Assembling a band in New York in October 1974, he rehearsed them over the course of a weekend, and then entered the studio to lay down 11 tracks within the space of just five days. He and the band knew the songs, so why spend more time than was absolutely necessary?

This was the way that John liked to work. Inspiration was usually the name of his game, and no Lennon-related project had ever taken so long to find its way into the record stores. To him, the LP's February 1975 release was, at the very least, a tremendous relief, almost as if some great weight had been lifted from his shoulders. To the critics and many members of the public, on the other hand, the record was little short of a rock 'n' roll masterpiece.

Gene Vincent was just one of many early
rockers who inspired John's love of
rock 'n' roll, and moved John to create
the *Rock 'n' Roll* album.

From left, Ronnie Bennett (Spector),
Estelle Bennett, and Nedra Talley, better
known as the Ronettes. Their 1963
recording of "Be My Baby" is timeless;
John's version is equally potent.

Although John was performing songs that had been around since he was 15, his arrangements of many of them were energetic and unique. Rather than simply retrace the steps taken by his teenage idols Chuck Berry, Buddy Holly, Little Richard, Gene Vincent, Larry Williams, and Sam Cooke, he had given the numbers a heavier, almost timeless feel. Songs that would have seemed dated in the hands of a lesser artist suddenly sounded fresh again, without ever straying from a full-blooded rock 'n' roll sound.

John's voice was as sharp as ever, and so were his instincts. It took natural intuition as well as great vision to transform the Ben E. King classic, "Stand By Me," into the rough-edged version that appears on this album, while the renditions of Chuck Berry's "Sweet Little Sixteen" and "You Can't Catch Me" are markedly different from the originals, but every bit as wonderful in their own way.

Yet perhaps the greatest performance of all was on one of the Spector-produced tracks that was judged unfit for inclusion on the record: a new version of the Ronettes' smash hit, "Be My Baby." Ironically, Spector had produced the original version in 1963. Now, he and John transformed what had been a celebratory girl-group love anthem into a hot 'n' heavy, out-and-out seduction number. Starting slowly, in a high-pitched, breathless voice, John sounds either high or laid-back beyond belief (or both), before building gradually to the song's climax, by which time he is literally screaming out the lyrics in a manner that can leave his "baby" in no doubt as to how he feels about her.

In several television, radio, and magazine interviews which he gave to promote the *Rock 'n' Roll* album, John talked about the new material he was putting together for his next record, and even went so far as to mention a TV show that

"Stepping Out . . . " John with a heavily pregnant Yoko, in New York in the fall of 1975. The impending birth filled John with pleasurable anticipation.

Opposite: "It's great to be legal again," John tells reporters after receiving his much fought-for Green Card at a special hearing in New York City on July 27, 1976. Having finally won his four-year battle to remain an American resident, John was informed by the judge that he would be able to apply for U.S. citizenship in 1981.

would be produced in connection with it. By this time, however, Yoko had become pregnant, and it soon became clear that John was putting his work on hold in anticipation of the great event.

On April 18, 1975, he made his last-ever stage appearance, singing "Slippin' and Slidin'" and "Imagine" in a performance that was broadcast on the June 13 television special, *Salute to Lew Grade.* On October 7 the New York State Supreme Court voted by two to one to reverse the deportation order against John, while instructing the Immigration Service to reconsider his request for resident status. Then, two days later, on John's 35th birthday, Yoko, at 42, gave birth to their only child, a son whom they named Sean Taro Ono Lennon.

The number nine had always been important to John: His birthday was on October 9; his mother had once lived at 9 Newcastle Road, Liverpool; Brian Epstein first saw the Beatles at the Cavern on November 9, 1961; he secured their EMI recording contract on May 9, 1962; and John first met Yoko on November 9, 1966. So it was that this lucky number also found its way into some of his song titles, such as "One After 909," "Revolution 9," and "#9 Dream." Now, with his son being born on the same day as himself, John saw the event as an omen; as the name, Lennon, derives from Ireland, he and Yoko decided to call the child Sean, the Irish version of John.

"I feel higher than the Empire State Building!" the ecstatic father told press journalists gathered outside the New York Hospital. Yet the birth had not been without its problems, for John had to call for a doctor when Yoko's body went into shock as a result of a transfusion of the wrong type of blood.

"I'm holding onto Yoko while this guy gets to the hospital room," John told *Playboy's* David Sheff in 1980. "He walks in, hardly notices that Yoko is going through convulsions, goes straight for me, smiles, shakes my hand, and says, 'I've always wanted to meet you, Mr. Lennon, I always enjoyed your music.' I start screaming: 'My wife's dying and you wanna talk about music!' Christ! A miracle that everything was okay."

Well aware that he had been less than a doting father to his

JOHN LENNON

John and Yoko in October of 1977, when they announced their decision to spend less time in the limelight and more time bringing up their two-year-old son. The fact that John was sporting a conventional hairstyle somehow helped fuel rumors that he was "going weird."

first son, Julian, John was determined to get it right the second time around. He and Yoko had waited a long time, and gone through a lot of heartache and pain, for their child to arrive, and John would now ensure that he – unlike both his father and himself in earlier years – would be fully involved in the boy's upbringing.

It was, therefore, convenient timing when the Beatles' contract with EMI Records expired on January 26, 1976. For the first time since 1962 John wasn't obliged to enter a recording studio, and the last time that he did so for four years was in April 1976, when he played piano on "Cookin' (In the Kitchen of Love)," a song that he had written especially for *Ringo's Rotogravure,* the new album by his old colleague.

During this same month, Freddie Lennon died of cancer at the age of 63. Just over five years earlier, shortly after John had undergone his primal therapy treatment, he had finally relieved himself of all the anger, pain, and frustration that he had bottled up since he was a child. In a hysterical screaming session John had told his shocked father exactly what he thought of him, of his desertion, and of his conveniently timed return. He had ordered him out of his house and out of his life. Freddie obliged, but during the last few days of his life he was back in constant touch with his son, via telephone calls made by John to the hospital in Brighton, England.

John later told interviewer David Sheff, "[Freddie] married a 22-year-old secretary that had been working for me or the Beatles, and had a child, which I thought was hopeful for a man who had lived a life of a drunk and almost a Bowery bum. A lot of his life was spent like that."

John's battle to remain in the United States reached a happy conclusion on July 27, when he was finally awarded his Green Card and told the press, "It's great to be legal again." It also meant that for the first time in five years he could travel abroad without fear of being refused re-entry. A few months after attending the inauguration gala of President Jimmy Carter in Washington D.C., John and Yoko, together with Sean, flew to Japan for an extended vacation. There they visited many of

The Dakota building, on the corner of West 72nd Street and Central Park West,
as glimpsed through the trees of Strawberry Fields, the section of park
dedicated to John's memory.

Yoko's relatives, and on October 4 they held a press conference at the Hotel Okura, at which John stated, "We've basically decided, without a great decision, to be with our baby as much as we can, until we feel we can take the time off to indulge ourselves creating things outside the family. Maybe when he's three, four, or five, then we'll think about creating something else other than the child."

In short, what this amounted to was that John would lead a fairly ordinary life, without venturing into the public spotlight, visiting clubs, going to parties, and so on. The press, of course, decided in no time at all that this was reason enough to dub him "The Howard Hughes of Rock." Over the next few years stories would constantly find their way into the papers, reporting on what were termed the Lennons' wild eccentricities: spending lavish amounts on properties dotted around the States, "extortionate" sums on special Regis Holstein cows for their Delaware farm, and keeping an entire apartment for

Yoko's fur coats in the Dakota building in New York.

John and Yoko had bought their sixth floor apartment in the Dakota, situated on the corner of West 72nd Street and Central Park West, in April of 1973. A gothic, somewhat eerie-looking building, this had been the setting for Roman Polanski's 1968 devil-worship horror film, *Rosemary's Baby;* what better place for a "recluse" to hide himself away in?

Yet, to all intents and purposes, what was actually going on behind these doors was hardly strange, let alone supernatural. Quite simply, the couple had decided to reverse roles: Yoko, the former avant-garde artist who had once turned her back on material wealth, now took care of the couple's business affairs.

She invested in properties, bought and sold artworks, and helped sort out the complicated financial and legal affairs in which the Beatles were still tangled up. This meant going to countless business meetings and having to combat the bullying

The 1975 Grammy Awards ceremony marked John and Yoko's first public appearance together after their 15-month separation. Art Garfunkel, Paul Simon, and Roberta Flack (barely visible) joined the couple backstage.

tactics of the men whom she faced around the tables. At first, this was a daunting task, but Yoko's adversaries gradually gained respect for her strong character and her sharp business brain. In time, she vastly expanded the overall value of the estate she shared with John.

John, on the other hand, had always been the archetypal "man's man," a hard rock 'n' roller who enjoyed the sexual pleasures offered by women, but who preferred to pursue work and other leisure interests in the company of like-minded male companions. All this had changed for a while after he teamed up with Yoko, but he later began to slip back into old habits, most notably during the infamous "Lost Weekend." Now, however, with no musical obligations to fulfill, and Yoko sitting down with the lawyers, accountants, and assorted financial sharks, he had plenty of spare time to enjoy new experiences for the first time since his mid-teens.

The number one priority in John's mind was Sean, and so while Yoko went out to work John stayed home and acted as a househusband, caring for the baby, preparing his meals and, later on, teaching him to read, write, and draw. For most men this kind of daily routine would be unusual, but in John's case it was downright peculiar. Cooking? The end-product was all that he had ever been interested in, not the preparation. Otherwise, when in doubt, with no woman about, open a can of beans!

It couldn't have been easy for John to dispense with this kind of attitude overnight, but he persisted. He forced himself to learn the basics in the kitchen; so proud was he of the first two loaves of bread that he baked, he couldn't resist taking a Polaroid photo of them.

In 1980, John described his bread to BBC interviewer Andy Peebles: "It looked great, you know, and it tasted good – that was pretty damned good – and so for about half a year, or a year, I was providing the food for Yoko, the baby . . . even the staff was eating! I was so excited that I could do it, that I would stop, bring all the staff in to eat lunch, you know. But after a bit it was wearing me out. . . . Okay, feed them, you don't get a gold record, they just swallow it, you know. If they swallow it, that means you were a hit, if they don't swallow it, that means you did something wrong. . . .

"They loved the bread. I'd make two on Fridays, supposed to last a week; it'd be gone Saturday afternoon, you know. Whoom! Like pigs – whoomph, it's gone. So I started buying the bread again, pretty damned quick!"

For all this effort, John also found plenty of time to indulge himself. On the one hand, this meant doing positive things such as traveling to places as far afield as Hong Kong or South Africa. On the other, it would simply be a case of enjoying one of his oldest hobbies: lazing around and drifting. A confirmed TV addict, he would spend days lying on top of his large bed, remote control in hand, flicking from channel to channel, watching anything from news bulletins and game shows, to old films or science-nature programs. He had also been an avid reader since childhood, and so he could now bury himself in as many books as he liked without having to worry about recording deadlines or sales promotion.

Later on John would say that throughout his four-year retirement he hung up his guitar and hardly gave a thought to music, but this was not strictly true. Certainly, to distance himself from the rock business, he most likely didn't listen to mainstream radio stations broadcasting the current chart hits or buy any of the latest records. But from evidence that has surfaced during the past few years, he definitely turned his hand to songwriting on numerous occasions, and even recorded demos of some of these compositions.

Furthermore, he also rediscovered other former favorite pastimes, and spent many hours making cartoon drawings, writing poems and, in a piece called "The Ballad of John and Yoko," documenting the different stages in his relationship

"Beautiful Boys": Father and son, in the kitchen at the Dakota, 1978.

"The center of the circle will always be our home. . . ." John, Sean, and Yoko—the "Three Virgins," as John liked to put it— together in 1978.

Through all the years of John's fame, Aunt Mimi kept the faith. John, wrapped up in fatherhood again and suddenly nostalgic, asked Mimi to send him drawings and other items from his own childhood.

with his wife. After his death, these would be collected and published in a volume called *Skywriting By Word of Mouth*.

In the book's afterword, Yoko recalled: "John wrote very quickly. Words flowed from his pen like sparkling spring water; he never had to stop to think. . . ."

At the same time, his deep involvement in raising a child also renewed his interest in his own early years, and on a few occasions he wrote to Aunt Mimi asking her to send him some of his old paintings, drawings, poetry, and school reports. Since the mid-1960s Mimi had been living in the waterfront bungalow that John had bought her in Poole, on the southern coast of England. There, packed away in cupboards and drawers, she kept many mementos of John's childhood, including his old school tie, which she happily sent to him when he requested it. This must have seemed ironic, considering how much John had hated wearing it in the first place!

In the *New York Times* of Sunday, May 27, 1979, a full-page advertisement appeared under the heading, "A Love Letter From John and Yoko. To People Who Ask Us What, When and Why." In it the couple explained what they had been doing during the past few years, and described their current situation:

"The house is getting very comfortable now. Sean is beautiful. The plants are growing. The cats are purring. The town is shining, sun, rain or snow."

The Lennons had found the contentment that had previously eluded them by simply living quietly together as a family, away from the prying eyes of the world outside. They appreciated the fact that people were still interested in what they were doing, and thanked those who respected the privacy that they felt they needed at this point.

"If you think of us next time, remember, our silence is a silence of love and not of indifference," they wrote, before signing off and adding a P.S.: "We noticed that three angels were looking over our shoulders when we wrote this!"

And who might this trio of winged wonders happen to be? Paul, George, and Ringo? If anything, this last line was just a typically Lennonish wind-up, but of course for many it just confirmed their suspicions of John's eccentricity. As if all this weren't evidence enough, a photo that appeared in newspapers at about that time showed that John had pulled his hair back in a pony tail and had grown a bushy beard and moustache. This "new" look – actually quite similar to John's appearance of ten years earlier – aroused comment at the same time that some fans were abuzz over a rumor that John had gone totally bald! One way or another, then, a certain proportion of Lennon-watchers was determined to believe that John was an oddball.

Yet the truth was quite the reverse. Having campaigned for peace in the world for so many years, John was, at last, at peace with himself. He adored his wife and child, was extremely happy with his way of life, and no longer felt the need to prove himself to anyone. The only conflict that he was suffering was staying out of public life altogether; in many ways he didn't miss the spotlight, but he sometimes felt awkward about going so far out of his way to avoid it.

In 1979, Paul Goresh was a New Jersey college student who would travel in to the big city to get a glimpse of John. On two occasions he had met him inside the Dakota by posing as a TV repairman, and now he would hang around outside the building with his $350 camera in the hope of taking some snaps of his idol. John, however, didn't want his face in the papers, and as a result Paul soon came face to face with the two sides of John's character.

"He thought I was working for the press," Goresh recalls. "He was really uptight about cameras, and he had asked me not to take pictures. I guess I was harassing him a little bit, but having already met him and got his autograph all I really wanted was some personal documentation. I wasn't planning on selling it or anything, and so I'd try to get pictures of him from across the street. But he spotted me and he was a little upset about that, and he came over and he tried to grab the camera. I had to push him away, and I told him, 'Don't do that, you're going to break my camera.' And he said, 'Well, I don't want any pictures!' I could see he was really upset and I felt

As married life grew sweeter, John and Yoko felt increasingly comfortable in New York, where fans respected their desire for privacy.

JOHN LENNON

"Every day in every way it's getting better and better." John and Yoko enjoy a stroll in Manhattan's Central Park in 1980.

terrible, because I really cared about him and I didn't want him to not like me. I said, 'I'm only a fan, John,' and he said, 'Well, if you're a fan, then give me the film!'"

Goresh was reluctant to give up the two shots that he had already taken, but as a token gesture he rewound the film and handed it to John, asking him to develop it for him and just give him the photos for his private collection. John's angered response was to expose the film there and then, saying, "I told you, no pictures," before storming off.

Later, however, John's assistant told Paul that John felt guilty about what he had done, and he wanted to make up for the incident. When John appeared he invited Paul to join him for a walk, explaining, "I really thought you worked for the press and you really scared me. I thought you were looking for some sort of scandal story, having already been in my home as a TV repairman." Now he realized this wasn't so. "As long as you don't bring a camera we won't have any problems."

Over the next year or so, the star and the fan would often go for walks together, "and although he didn't want to be noticed, the guy would walk down Columbus Avenue wearing a blue, black and white checkered jacket, with a straw hat and big sunglasses," recalls Paul. "I would say to him, 'I think you're pretty noticeable like this, John,' and he would just laugh.

"He was so bright and witty, and he was so personable. When I was with him I was in awe of him, but he made me feel so at ease, and he treated me as if I was his equal. And I was always impressed with that, because this guy would honestly rather talk about you than himself, and it was sincere. He would laugh and joke, and I'd get on his nerves sometimes talking about the Beatles so much, but he would still be able to laugh at me because he knew what it was to be a fan."

In August of 1980, after returning from a trip to Bermuda, John informed Paul Goresh that he was about to resume his recording career. Yoko, who stayed behind in New York to deal with business, was very influenced by astrology and numerology. She would read her tarot cards and often tell John when the time was right to do certain things. This included advice about making journeys to particular destinations, and John would follow such decisions without questioning their wisdom; *Rolling Stone's The Ballad of John and Yoko* relates that John once told close friend Elliot Mintz, "She will say things you will not understand. Go with it. She's always right."

For the Bermuda trip John had set sail on his new 65-foot yacht, and en route took time to listen to cassette tapes of contemporary artists such as the Pretenders, the B-52s, Madness, and Lene Lovich (whom he referred to as "Lenny Loveritch"). He suddenly realized that much of the new music wasn't a million miles away from the kind of material that he and Yoko had been performing ten years before. This was confirmed when he arrived in Bermuda and, together with his assistant Fred Seaman, visited some discos for the first time in years and heard sounds – such as the B-52s' "Rock Lobster" – which reminded him of Yoko's earlier work.

For a few months John had slowly been regaining his interest in popular music. Now it was full-blown again, and in a sudden burst of inspiration he wrote a batch of new songs in a very short space of time. Each time he completed a piece, he would phone Yoko in New York and tell her about it. She, in turn, would write a song that responded to John's lyrics, and after a while their compositions formed a sort of dialogue.

In the meantime, Sean and his nanny had flown out to Bermuda to meet John, and each day father and son would go swimming and sightseeing together. On one occasion, while taking a tour around a botanical garden, John was fascinated by the name of an orchid – Double Fantasy. This, to him, summed up the relationship he shared with Yoko, as well as that between men and women in general. It would, he thought, be an ideal title for an album.

Following John's return to New York, he and Yoko recruited many top session musicians and technicians, and booked studio time at the Hit Factory. John now felt ready to make his re-entry into public life, for as he himself expressed it to *Newsweek* interviewer Barbara Graustark, "*This* housewife would like to have a career for a bit!"

By the summer of 1980, at ease with himself and happy with his family, John was ready to make music again.

CHAPTER 14

STEPPING OUT

"I always consider my work one piece . . . and I consider that my work won't be finished until I'm dead and buried, and I hope that's a long, long time."

JOHN LENNON
December 8, 1980 – the last day of his life
(RKO Radio interview)

Opposite: As John neared his fortieth birthday in 1980, he was happily married, at peace with himself, and eager to return to his music. His fans rejoiced; John's future seemed limitless.

"(Just Like) Starting Over" was the only single released off the *Double Fantasy* album during John's lifetime. "Woman" (*above*) and "Watching the Wheels" (*below*) followed his death. The latter single boasted a cover photo by Lennon fan Paul Goresh.

After they resumed their commercial recording career on August 4, 1980, John and Yoko went public again. They started giving magazine interviews, announced that they had signed a deal with Geffen Records, and on October 9, in celebration of John's 40th birthday and Sean's 5th, Yoko even went so far as to pay for an airplane to sky-write, "Happy Birthday John + Sean. Love Yoko," over New York City.

This followed the 500 fresh gardenias and diamond heart that John had given his wife, and the vintage Rolls-Royce that he had received from her, when toasting their 11th wedding anniversary at their home in West Palm Beach earlier in the year. The scene was one of domestic bliss, which was the underlying theme presented to the world when the *Double Fantasy* album was released in November.

The record contained seven tracks by John alternating with seven by Yoko, and to them it didn't matter if this arrangement didn't suit all ears. It was the only way that John wanted to work. As he himself had put it during an RKO Radio interview on the last day of his life, "There's only two artists that I've ever worked with for more than a one-night stand, as it were: That's Paul McCartney and Yoko Ono, and I think that's a pretty damned good choice!"

John's songs reasserted his great musical talents: his versatility as a composer, his ability to communicate, and the strength and passion of his unique voice. "(Just Like) Starting Over," the aptly titled first single to be released off the album, was a catchy pop number that borrowed some of its style and feel from the '50s, prompting John to refer to it as his "Elvis Orbison" track. In "I'm Losing You," on the other hand, all of the old demons surface, with John – his voice full of pain and aggression – expressing his feelings of insecurity and isolation when staying in Bermuda, and unable to reach Yoko on the telephone. Clearly, however contented he now was, some things still never changed.

Yet this cut was an exception to the new rule, and the rest of the *Double Fantasy* material really describes how John was learning to come to terms with himself. "It is the most violent people who go for love and peace," he told *Playboy*'s David Sheff at around this time. "Everything's the opposite. But I sincerely believe in love and peace. I am a violent man who has learned not to be violent and regrets his violence."

John also felt bad about the way he had treated many of the women in his life; he often had adopted a tough stance in order to disguise his own insecurity. He told Sheff that he had been "trying to cover up the feminine side, which I still have a tendency to do, but I'm learning. I'm learning that it's all right to be soft and allow that side of me out."

So it is that John's song "Woman" opens with a quote from Chairman Mao, "For the other half of the sky," signifying that this love song is dedicated to all women, not only his wife:

> "Woman, I can hardly express
> My mixed emotions at my thoughtlessness
> After all I'm forever in your debt"

Tender lyrics, an evocative melody, and a wonderful vocal performance mark "Woman" – which John referred to as the album's "Beatle track" – as John Lennon at his very best. Three and a half minutes of pure magic, it was written by John in Bermuda in only 15 minutes.

John harkened back to the time in Bermuda with "Watching the Wheels," in which he describes his years spent as a homebody and househusband, while in "Beautiful Boy (Darling Boy)," a song directed at Sean, he muses:

> "I can hardly wait
> to see you come of age
> But I guess we'll both
> just have to be patient"

John was interested in every stage of his young son's development, for as he said to *Playboy*'s David Sheff: "He didn't come out of my belly but, by God, I made his bones, because I've attended to every meal, and to how he sleeps, and to the fact that he swims like a fish . . . I'm so proud of those things. He is my biggest pride, you see."

Above and below: The sleeves of two singles culled from the posthumously released *Milk & Honey* album, both sporting photographs taken inside the Dakota in September of 1980.

JOHN LENNON

John was always happy to oblige fans who asked for his autograph. On the last
day of his life, this generous accessibility would be cruelly exploited.

"Beautiful Boy (Darling Boy)," while concerning itself with Sean, also ends with a sentiment that turned out to be cruelly prophetic for John:

> "Life is what happens to you
> while you're busy
> making other plans"

Completely bitten by the work bug, John and Yoko had already laid down studio demo tracks for most of the material on their next album, and were even looking ahead to the one after that and a subsequent world tour. But fate intervened, and the record that was tentatively titled *Milk and Honey* was held back until several years after John's death. When it was eventually released, in January of 1984, it revealed just how much John still had to offer, and how badly the world had been deprived by his passing.

Tracks such as "I'm Stepping Out" and "Nobody Told Me" display all of his old humor, and in "I Don't Wanna Face It" he sends up those who pester him about taking up causes that they themselves don't truly believe in:

> "Say you're looking
> for some peace and love
> Leader of a big old band
> You wanna save humanity
> But it's people that
> you just can't stand"

The album's "Borrowed Time" describes the pain and confusion of John's youth, and his pleasure at growing older, but if the line about him "Living on borrowed time" strikes an ironic chord, this is as nothing to a song which was originally intended for *Double Fantasy* but wasn't recorded in time for the pre-Christmas deadline. The song was "Grow Old With Me," which took its inspiration, and its opening two lines, from a poem by Robert Browning. John envisaged the song as a standard; one that could be sung at church weddings. Yet, by the time of his death, he had taped it only a few times at home on a cassette recorder, singing and playing the piano, backed by a beat coming out of a rhythm box. It was the last of these recordings that Yoko included on the *Milk and Honey* album.

Having opened with Browning's words – "Grow old along with me, The best is yet to be" – John closes the song with:

> "Grow old along with me
> Whatever fate decrees
> We will see it through
> For our love is true
> God bless our love"

Looking fit and healthy at 40, having given up alcohol, dangerous drugs, meat, and even sugar (but not high-tar cigarettes or extra-black coffee), John was in a buoyant mood on December 6 as he and Yoko spoke to Andy Peebles for an interview on BBC Radio. Talking about their past, present, and a future that was bright with promise, John described how he loved the freedom of living almost like an ordinary citizen in New York, without being harassed by fans:

"I've been walking the streets for the last seven years. . . . I can go right out this door now and go in a restaurant. You want to know how great that is? Or go to the movies? I mean, people come up and ask for autographs or say 'Hi,' but they won't bug you!"

On the morning of December 8, sitting in the Lenono office at the Dakota, John, together with Yoko, gave his last-ever interview. This was done for RKO Radio, in the presence of Dave Sholin, Laurie Kaye, Ron Hummel, and Bert Keane. "I still believe in love, peace, I still believe in positive thinking," he told them. "You have to give thanks to God, or whatever it is up there, the fact that we all survived. We all survived

"Our love is still special. . . ." John and Yoko intended to use one of the results of this November 1980 photo session for their Christmas card that year.

John and Yoko share a moment at one of the pianos inside the Dakota, September 1980. The couple planned a full-scale world tour after the proposed release of their second "comeback" album in 1981.

Vietnam or Watergate or the tremendous upheaval of the world. . . . The whole map's changed and we're going into an unknown future, but we're still all here, and while there's life there's hope."

A few days earlier, John had his hair cut in a style similar to that which he had sported as a Teddy boy all those years ago, and this is how he appeared in snapshots with the BBC team on December 6, and in the photos taken by Annie Leibovitz inside the Dakota throughout the afternoon of the 8th. In some shots with Yoko, intended for the cover of *Rolling Stone,* he even posed naked once again. It was almost as if John had come full circle.

Meanwhile, Yoko's new song, "Walking On Thin Ice," was being mixed at the Hit Factory. At around 4:15 p.m., as the two of them left for the studio, John was met outside the Dakota by Paul Goresh, who proceeded to show him some of the photos that he had recently taken of the couple. Another fan, named Mark David Chapman, was standing nearby. Born in Fort Worth, Texas, but now living in Hawaii, Chapman had flown to New York with the specific aim of coming face to face with John Lennon.

Paul Goresh remembers, "I was on John's right, and he was looking at the pictures and asking me to bring some more shots that I had taken six days earlier. As we were in the middle of this conversation, Chapman came up on John's left and he just held the [*Double Fantasy*] album out. I didn't even hear him say anything. John turned and looked at him, and he was just holding the album with two hands, and John said, 'Do you want that signed?' and Chapman nodded. John took the album, and then he looked at me as if to say, 'What, can't he speak?' you know, 'This is strange,' but it didn't mean anything at the time.

"As John started to sign the album I just happened to have my camera ready, and so I stepped back and took a picture of him signing the cover; I didn't even want the other guy in the picture! After that, I took a shot of John turning to Chapman, holding the album out and asking, 'Is that all right?' Chapman

Listening to a playback during a mixing session for the *Double Fantasy* album
at the Hit Factory, New York, in September of 1980. John always liked
to work quickly: Recording had begun on August 4;
just over three months later the record was in the shops.

nodded, took the album and just backed away without even turning, and so in the next picture that I took John's eyebrows are raised, as if to say, 'That's strange!'

"In all, I shot seven or eight frames, and the last picture is of John's profile as he was getting into the limousine. That turned out to be the last picture of John alive."

Outside the entrance arch to the Dakota there is a small brass-colored booth, manned 24 hours a day by a blue-uniformed guard who opens the tall iron security gates for residents and their guests. After John's car had driven away, Chapman pointed out to both the guard, Jose Perdomo, and to Paul Goresh, that he was placing his autographed album behind the booth. At the time, unfortunately, neither Perdomo nor Goresh realized the cryptic, evil significance of this.

"I said to him, 'What are you putting it there for?'" recalls Paul. "And he said, 'Well, I'm just showing you guys where it is, because you'll want to know where it is later.' That's what he said. . . ."

At around 8:30 p.m. Paul decided to go home, but Chapman urged him to stay. "I said, 'What for?' and he said, 'Well, something might happen and you might never see him again, and then you won't get his autograph.' I said, 'Listen, I don't need to wait for John's autograph, I speak to him all the time. And besides, what's going to happen?' He then realized what he'd been saying and he kinda pulled himself together and said, 'Oh well, I was just thinking that he might go to Spain tonight or something!'"

Mark Chapman would later be diagnosed by psychiatrists as a paranoid schizophrenic – someone who had come to imagine that he himself was John Lennon, and who was only prevented from assuming this role on a full-time basis by the existence of the man himself. Others assert that he was simply a madman looking to make a name for himself, and there has even been a wild theory in which Chapman is linked to the CIA – a hit man hired to do away with a re-emerging star who had caused political unrest in the past.

JOHN LENNON

233

December 8, 1980: Following John's assassination, people gather behind police
barricades outside the main entrance to the Dakota building.

Whatever the truth of the matter, when John returned with Yoko at around 10:50 that night, Chapman was waiting for him in the shadows of the entrance archway. Instead of driving straight through this passage into the Dakota's courtyard, John and Yoko would often have the driver stop by the sidewalk so that they could greet fans as they walked in. On this occasion they did it once too often.

As they stepped from the car, Yoko following behind her husband, a voice called out "Mr. Lennon!" John, turning to see who was asking for him, was met with a barrage of gunfire as Chapman – squatting in a combat stance – emptied his .38-caliber gun and pumped four bullets into John's back and left arm. A fifth one missed. John, amazingly, continued to stagger forward and up the steps into the office of the Dakota night man, Jay Hastings, still clutching the tapes from that

evening's studio session. Eyes glazed, and with a look of total shock on his face, he said to Hastings, "Help me . . . I've been shot. . . ." before collapsing face-first on the floor, blood pouring from his mouth and chest (some of the bullets had exited through the front of his body, creating seven visible wounds).

As Hastings helped Yoko tend to her dying husband – covering him in his uniform jacket and removing John's glasses – Chapman calmly stood on the sidewalk outside, reading a copy of his favorite book, *The Catcher in the Rye*. "Do you know what you've just done?" Jose Perdomo screamed at him. "Yes," came the reply, "I've shot John Lennon."

John's body was limp, his bones shattered, as police officers lifted him into a car. On the way to Roosevelt Hospital, Officer James Moran attempted to keep him in the land of the living

After John had been pronounced dead at New York's Roosevelt Hospital, Yoko
returned to the Lennon-Ono apartment at the Dakota. Outside, people gathered
on West 72nd Street, and throughout the pre-dawn hours of December 9 Yoko
could hear them singing "All You Need Is Love" and "Give Peace a Chance."

by yelling, "Do you know who you are?" John moaned and nodded his head, as if to say "Yes," but he had no chance of survival. A team of seven doctors labored to save him at the hospital, but Dr. Stephan Lynn later announced that he had been "dead on arrival," due to massive loss of blood caused by "a significant injury of the major vessels inside the chest." The official time of death was given as 11:07 p.m.

John himself would have been quick to spot the significant part that the number nine was now playing in his death just as it had during his lifetime: The combination of figures in 11:07 adds up to the magic total, the Roosevelt Hospital is situated on Ninth Street, and in Britain, where the time is five hours ahead of that in New York, he died just after 4:00 a.m. on December 9.

Aunt Mimi, Paul McCartney, George Harrison, and Cynthia and Julian Lennon were awakened from their sleep to be informed of the tragedy, while in America some television and radio broadcasters openly cried on the air as they broke the news to a stunned nation. Ringo, vacationing in Bermuda with future wife Barbara Bach, immediately flew to New York to see Yoko and Sean.

On December 10, John's body was cremated, and at 2:00 p.m. EST on Sunday, December 14, some 400,000 people gathered in New York's Central Park to join the rest of the world in ten minutes' silence for his memory. "John loved and prayed for the human race," said Yoko. "Please do the same for him."

"Mahatma Gandhi and Martin Luther King are great examples of fantastic non-violents who died violently," John had asserted just three months earlier to *Playboy*'s David Sheff. "I can never work that out. We're pacifists, but I'm not sure what it

John's fans were stunned and saddened by his violent, needless death. The
shock and sense of loss is apparent on the faces of these grieving
New Yorkers. The irony was staggering: John Lennon, a man of peace,
had been cut down by a gunman's bullet at the age of 40.

JOHN LENNON

At 2:00 p.m. EST on Sunday, December 14, 1980, people around the world—
including 400,000 gathered in New York's Central Park—
observed ten minutes' silence in respect to John's memory.
The man was gone, but the music would live on.

means when you're such a pacifist that you get shot. I can never understand that."

Nobody could. In the Soviet Union, the newspaper representing the Communist Youth League stated that it was "a bitter irony that a man who devoted his songs and music to the struggle against violence, should become a victim of violence."

In America, a fan named Jon Grabill wrote a letter to *Rolling Stone* magazine, observing that "We've come a long way in seventeen years, from shooting presidents to murdering musicians."

In the White House, President Jimmy Carter said, "John Lennon helped create the mood and the music of the time," while the Beatles' New York concert promoter, Sid Bernstein, described John as "the Bach, Beethoven, the Rachmaninoff of our time."

"It was a staggering moment when I heard the news," said Frank Sinatra, the musical idol of a previous generation. "Lennon was a most talented man and, above all, a gentle soul."

Paul McCartney, looking pale and drawn, told journalists, "I can't take it in. John was a great man who'll be remembered for his unique contributions to art, music, and world peace." George Harrison, meanwhile, said that he was "stunned. To rob life is the greatest robbery."

But for all the words of sorrow, praise, and anger, perhaps the most accurate assessment was that made by author Norman Mailer: "We have," he asserted, "lost a genius of the spirit."

A world normally divided in opinion was now united in its grief and condemnation of such a violent ending for a man who had preached love and peace, and given hope and pleasure to millions. For one brief, poignant moment, John Lennon's dream of global unity had come true.

JOHN LENNON

CHAPTER 15

NOW AND FOREVER

*"Well we all shine on
Like the moon
and the stars
and the sun"*

JOHN LENNON
"Instant Karma!" (1970)

Opposite: Gone but never forgotten: The Strawberry Fields section of New York's Central Park was instigated by Yoko to commemorate John's life and work, and was officially opened by her, together with John's sons Julian and Sean, on October 9, 1985. Strawberry Fields' mosaic centerpiece (*top*) bears a message that just about says it all.

Second-generation recording artist Julian Lennon has learned since his father's death that to be the son of a legend—as well as to bear a striking physical resemblance to him—brings both advantages and drawbacks.

In a 1987 interview conducted by this writer with the Beatles' record producer, George Martin, he said, "As far as the music was concerned, John Lennon was always looking for the impossible, the unattainable. He was never satisfied. He once said to me, in one of our evenings together when we were reminiscing, 'You know, George, I've never really liked anything we've ever done.' I said, 'Really, John? But you made some fantastic records!' He said, 'Well, if I could do them all over again, I would.'"

Few, it appears, tend to agree with John's view about his own work, and since his death his records – those he did with and without the Beatles – have continued to sell in vast quantities around the globe. The purchasers have been a mixture of the old and the new: faithful fans, replacing worn-out copies with vinyl, tape, or compact disc; and a generation of younger people who have come to hear and appreciate John's music for the first time.

What they listen to is the work of a singular talent, a man who composed songs – great songs – in styles spanning the whole range of popular music, and that provide not only tremendous enjoyment but also great insight into John's thoughts and experiences. The techniques employed in many of the earlier recordings may now sound dated, but the performances themselves are timeless, as fresh and as full of energy, heart, and soul as when John and his colleagues first worked on them.

Since 1980, there have been countless attempts – made, more often than not, by members of the press and other media – to either deify or vilify John; all have been wildly inaccurate. John, as he himself was always the first to admit, was by no means an angel, and he would have had little time for those who have set him up as some kind of a god. He had enough trouble putting up with that during his lifetime, and he always urged people, both through his spoken comments and through his music, to pursue their own dreams and not rely on leadership figures. As he expressed it in the song "I Found Out" in 1970:

Sean and Yoko, coping with the grief and doing their best to see that John
remains properly celebrated and a vital part of his fans' lives.

"Now that I showed you
what I been through
Don't take nobody's word
what you can do
There ain't no Jesus
gonna come from the sky. . . ."

But if John was no god, neither was he the devil that cynical
biographers and other people would have him be. His extraordinary talent aside, John was in most respects just a regular
human being, with strengths and weaknesses like anyone else.
Many of the things he did wouldn't have won him any medals
for socially acceptable behavior but, as those who really
knew him always confirm, his good points – his honesty, his
generosity, his sensitivity, his wit, and his lack of conceit – far
outweighed the bad.

Inevitably, though, a person who is not around to defend
himself is easy meat for the cash-in merchants and rumor-

JOHN LENNON

JOHN LENNON

mongers. Some of the John Lennon stories that have surfaced since his death are emphatic enough to have booked him a permanent place in either Heaven or Hell. At the same time, what many of the tales have lacked in offensiveness they have made up for in sheer stupidity. One story involved a woman who claimed to have been contacted by John from beyond the grave in order to write more hit songs on his behalf. Another one revolved around a pet parrot called Sergeant Pepper, who (his owner claimed) had once been owned by John and had memorized some of his unreleased compositions. The feathered birdbrain, which had apparently been purchased by the human one for a mere $400,000 at auction, was happy to squawk its way through 20 never-before-heard Lennon masterpieces, and these noises were being written down as sheet music by a self-styled composer. The result was to be an album of orchestra music, entitled *The Lost Works of John Lennon*. The world is still waiting!

In all, John has proved to be as big a business property in death as he was in life. But unlike other music celebrities who met sudden deaths, he did not need to die in order to provide a boost to his career. During his last few months he gave the world a healthy taste of his unique talent. He was cut off during a period of intense creativity, one signaling that he still had many more years of valuable music to offer his public.

While we had the opportunity to enjoy only half of John Lennon's potential life's work, and are likely to wonder what the second half may have brought, such speculation is frustrating and, in the end, useless. What we do know is that the inheritance we have been left is rich in both quality and quantity, and can be shared by all people and passed on, intact, from generation to generation.

Shortly before his death, in a *Playboy* interview in which he reflected on years of challenge, celebrity, and creativity, John said, "I've done more in my life than most people would do in ten." He was absolutely right. The man has gone, but his music is immortal.

In October of 1988, tying in with the release of the documentary film *Imagine: John Lennon,* John finally achieved recognition on Hollywood Boulevard's Walk of Fame as one of the world's greatest recording artists.

Opposite: The Beatles Shop in Mathew Street, Liverpool, situated just a few yards from the original site of The Cavern Club, caters to a demand that may never diminish.

JOHN LENNON

A bit of the music the world loved best.

JOHN LENNON'S RECORDED WORK

Including 220 songs that he wrote or co-wrote

RECORDINGS WITH THE BEATLES

The following is a complete list of John's released recordings with the Beatles. Those printed in **boldface** are the ones that he either composed on his own, or in whose composition he played a significant role. The titles in *italics* are of recordings composed by people outside of the group, on which John sang the lead vocal. The songs in standard typeface are ones that he did not write, but simply played an instrument on or sang backing vocals. To some of these he may have contributed a word, phrase, or idea, but not enough to credit the number as truly his.

Songs are listed in chronological order, according to the year of their initial release, not the order in which they were written or recorded.

NOTE: Beatles numbers which John did not write or help to record are not listed here.

1963

Please Please Me; Ask Me Why; Misery; *Anna (Go to Him); Baby It's You;* **Do You Want to Know A Secret; There's a Place;** *Twist and Shout;* **From Me to You; Thank You Girl; She Loves You; I'll Get You; I Want to Hold Your Hand; This Boy; It Won't Be Long; All I've Got to Do; Little Child;** *Please Mr. Postman; You Really Got a Hold on Me;* **I Wanna Be Your Man; Not a Second Time;** *Money (That's What I Want)*

I Saw Her Standing There; Chains; Boys; A Taste of Honey

1962

Love Me Do; P.S. I Love You

1964

Cry for a Shadow; *Ain't She Sweet;* **You Can't Do That; I Call Your Name;** *Slow Down;* **A Hard Day's Night; I Should Have Known Better; If I Fell; I'm Happy Just to Dance with You; Tell Me Why; Any Time at All; I'll Cry Instead; When I Get Home; I'll Be Back; I Feel Fine; No Reply; I'm a Loser; Baby's in Black;** *Rock and Roll Music; Mr. Moonlight;* **Eight Days a Week;** *Words of Love;* **Every Little Thing; I Don't Want to Spoil the Party; What You're Doing**

Can't Buy Me Love; Long Tall Sally; Matchbox; Things We Said Today; And I Love Her; She's a Woman; I'll Follow the Sun; Kansas City/Hey-Hey-Hey-Hey!; Honey Don't; Everybody's Trying to Be My Baby

1965

Ticket to Ride; Yes It Is; Help!; You've Got to Hide Your Love Away; You're Going to Lose That Girl; It's Only Love; *Dizzy Miss Lizzy;* **Day Tripper; We Can Work It Out; Drive My Car; Norwegian Wood (This Bird Has Flown); Nowhere Man; The Word; What Goes On; Girl; In My Life; Wait; Run for Your Life**

I'm Down; The Night Before; I Need You; Another Girl; Act Naturally; You Like Me Too Much; Tell Me What You See; I've Just Seen a Face; You Won't See Me; Think For Yourself; Michelle; I'm Looking Through You; If I Needed Someone

1966

Rain; Eleanor Rigby; Taxman; I'm Only Sleeping; She Said She Said; And Your Bird Can Sing; Doctor Robert; Tomorrow Never Knows; *Bad Boy*

Paperback Writer; Yellow Submarine; Here, There and Everywhere; Good Day Sunshine; I Want to Tell You; Got to Get You Into My Life

1967

Strawberry Fields Forever; With a Little Help from My Friends; Lucy in the Sky with Diamonds; Getting Better; She's Leaving Home; Being for the Benefit of Mr. Kite!; Good Morning, Good Morning; A Day in the Life; All You Need is Love; Baby You're a Rich Man; I Am the Walrus; Flying

Penny Lane; Sgt. Pepper's Lonely Hearts Club Band; Fixing a Hole; When I'm Sixty-Four; Sgt. Pepper's Lonely Hearts Club Band (Reprise); Hello, Goodbye; Magical Mystery Tour; Your Mother Should Know; The Fool on the Hill; Blue Jay Way

1968

Revolution; Dear Prudence; Glass Onion; The Continuing Story of Bungalow Bill; Happiness is a Warm Gun; I'm So Tired; Julia; Yer Blues; Everybody's Got Something to Hide (Except Me and My Monkey); Sexy Sadie; Revolution 1; Cry Baby Cry; Revolution 9; Good Night

Lady Madonna; The Inner Light; Hey Jude; Back in the USSR; Ob-La-Di, Ob-La-Da; While My Guitar Gently Weeps; Piggies; Rocky Racoon; I Will; Birthday; Helter Skelter; Honey Pie

1969

Hey Bulldog; Don't Let Me Down; The Ballad of John and Yoko; Come Together; I Want You (She's So Heavy); Because; Sun King; Mean Mr. Mustard; Polythene Pam; Across the Universe

Only a Northern Song; All Together Now; It's All Too Much; Get Back; Old Brown Shoe; Something; Maxwell's Silver Hammer; Oh! Darling; Octopus's Garden; You Never Give Me Your Money; She Came in Through the Bathroom Window; The End

1970

You Know My Name (Look Up the Number); Dig a Pony; Dig It; *Maggie May;* **I've Got a Feeling; One After 909**

Let It Be; Two Of Us; The Long and Winding Road; For You Blue

Unreleased songs that John recorded in the studio with the Beatles include:

How Do You Do It?; Leave My Kitten Alone; **If You've Got Trouble; What's the New Mary Jane**

Besame Mucho; That Means a Lot; Not Guilty

JOHN LENNON'S SOLO RECORDINGS

Titles printed in **boldface** are John's solo recordings of songs written by him. Titles printed in *italics* are John's solo recordings of songs written by other artists.

Albums such as *Unfinished Music No. 1: Two Virgins, Unfinished Music No. 2: Life with the Lions,* and *The Wedding Album* contain conceptual, avant-garde recordings, and the individual tracks are therefore not listed below as separate Lennon compositions.

The same applies to three of the live recordings on the *Some Time in New York City* album, and the "Nutopian International Anthem" – which is totally silent – on the *Mind Games* album.

JOHN LENNON'S RECORDED WORK

(The aforementioned "Revolution 9" was given the benefit of the doubt!)

1969

Give Peace a Chance; Cold Turkey

1970

Instant Karma!; Mother; Hold On; I Found Out; Working Class Hero; Isolation; Remember; Love; Well Well Well; Look at Me; God; My Mummy's Dead

1973

Mind Games; Meat City; Tight A$; Aisumasen (I'm Sorry); One Day (At a Time); Bring on the Lucie (Freda People); Intuition; Out the Blue; Only People; I Know (I Know); You Are Here

1971

Power to the People; Do the Oz; Imagine; Crippled Inside; Jealous Guy; It's So Hard; I Don't Want to Be a Soldier; Give Me Some Truth; Oh My Love; How Do You Sleep?; How?; Oh Yoko!; Happy Xmas (War is Over)

1974

Whatever Gets You Thru the Night; Beef Jerky; Going Down on Love; Old Dirt Road; What You Got; Bless You; Scared; #9 Dream; Surprise, Surprise (Sweet Bird of Paradox); Steel and Glass; Nobody Loves You (When You're Down and Out); *Ya Ya*

1975

1972

Woman is the Nigger of the World; Attica State; New York City; Sunday Bloody Sunday; The Luck of the Irish; John Sinclair; Angela; *Well (Baby Please Don't Go)*

Move Over Ms. L; *Be-Bop-A-Lula; Stand By Me; Rip It Up; Ready Teddy; You Can't Catch Me; Ain't That a Shame; Do You Want to Dance; Sweet Little Sixteen; Slippin' and Slidin'; Peggy Sue; Bring It on Home to Me; Send Me Some Lovin'; Bony Moronie; Ya Ya* (differs from John's 1974 version); *Just Because*

1980

(Just Like) Starting Over; Cleanup Time; I'm Losing You; Beautiful Boy (Darling Boy); Watching the Wheels; Woman; Dear Yoko

POSTHUMOUS RELEASES

1984

I'm Stepping Out; I Don't Wanna Face It; Nobody Told Me; Borrowed Time; (Forgive Me) My Little Flower Princess; Grow Old with Me; *Every Man Has a Woman Who Loves Him*

1986

Here We Go Again; Rock 'n' Roll People; *Angel Baby; Since My Baby Left Me; To Know Her is to Love Her*

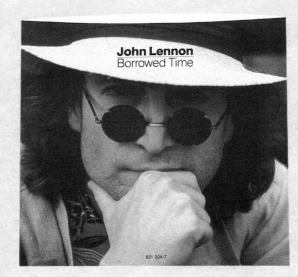

1988

Real Love

Since John's death, many other recordings – some, studio outtakes; others, just home or studio demos – have come to light. Among these are numerous complete and original compositions that were never commercially released during his lifetime. They include the following songs (titles that are variations and prototypes of other songs, as well as ideas with which John was simply playing around, are not listed):

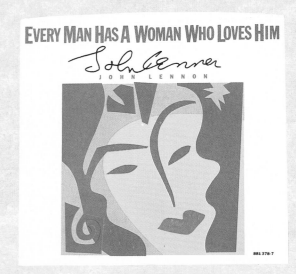

Across the River; Boat Song; Call My Name; A Case of the Blues; Dear John; Don't Be Afraid; Dream Time; Free as a Bird; Gone from This Place; The Happy Rishikesh Song; He Got the Blues; Help Me to Help Myself; Hold On, I'm Coming; I Ain't Got Time; I Don't Want to Lose You; I Promise; I Watch Your Face; Life Begins at Forty; The Maharishi Song; Man is Half of Woman (Woman is Half of Man); Mirror Mirror (On the Wall); Not for Love Nor Money; One of the Boys; Pill; Pop is the Name of the Game; Sally and Billy; Serve Yourself; She is a Friend of Dorothy's; Tennessee; Whatever Happened to . . .?; When a Boy Meets a Girl; You Saved My Soul with Your True Love

As a musician, John also made numerous guest appearances on records by other artists, including the Rolling Stones (We Love You), David Bowie (**Fame** and **Across the Universe**), Elton John (**One Day at a Time** and **Lucy in the Sky with Diamonds**), Harry Nilsson (Pussy Cats), David Peel and the Lower East Side (The Pope Smokes Dope), Elephants Memory (Elephants Memory), and all of Yoko Ono's singles and albums prior to 1981.

SONGS WRITTEN OR CO-WRITTEN BY JOHN FOR RELEASE BY OTHER ARTISTS

1963

Bad to Me (recorded by Billy J. Kramer and the Dakotas)
Hello Little Girl (recorded by the Fourmost)
I'm in Love (recorded by the Fourmost)

1971

God Save Us (recorded by Bill Elliott and the Elastic Oz Band)

1972

The Ballad of New York City (recorded by David Peel and the Lower East Side)

1973

I'm the Greatest (recorded by Ringo Starr)

1974

(It's All Da-Da Down To) Goodnight Vienna (recorded by Ringo Starr)
Mucho Mungo (recorded by Harry Nilsson)
Rock 'n' Roll People (recorded by Johnny Winter)

1975

Fame (recorded by David Bowie)

1976

Cookin' (In the Kitchen of Love) (recorded by Ringo Starr)

Photo Credits:

Front cover: Iain MacMillan Lenono Photo Archive

Back cover: Bob Freeman/Retna, Ltd.

Additional Copyright Information